rules
for the
unruly

RULES FOR THE UNRULY

LIVING AN UNCONVENTIONAL LIFE

MARION WINIK

a FIRESIDE BOOK

PUBLISHED BY SIMON & SCHUSTER

NEW YORK   LONDON   TORONTO   SYDNEY   SINGAPORE

FIRESIDE
Rockefeller Center
1230 Avenue of the Americas
New York, NY 10020

FIRESIDE and colophon are registered trademarks
of Simon & Schuster, Inc.

Designed by Diane Hobbing of SNAPHAUS GRAPHICS

Manufactured in the United States of America

10   9   8   7   6   5   4   3   2   1

Library of Congress Cataloging-in-Publication Data
Winik, Marion.
Rules for the unruly : living an unconventional
life / Marion Winik.
    p.   cm.
  1. Youth—Conduct of life.
BJ1661.W56 2001
170'.44—dc21

ISBN 0-7432-1603-2

for CRISPIN SARTWELL,
my ROLE MODEL.

Local conditions always put a limit on what an observer can see. Faint stars become lost in the glow of city lights. Heavy traffic on a nearby street may cause a star image to shiver. If the telescope is pointed at a planet that appears just over a neighbor's roof, heated air rising from the roof may turn the planet's image into a "boiling" blob. Gusts of wind, clouds suddenly rolling in, and inconveniently located trees are other hazards.

The observer with a broad open horizon, free from interfering lights, is lucky.

R. NEWTON MAYALL, MARGARET MAYALL,
AND JEROME WYCKOFF,
THE SKY OBSERVER'S GUIDE

contents

contents

IntRODUCtION

In all the time since that excellent June afternoon when I screeched out of my high school's parking lot after graduation, I never expected or hoped to see the place again. As you probably know, few bullets have more momentum than a departing senior. Yet here I was, ricocheting back twenty-five years later, and did it feel weird. First of all, the place looked exactly the same: the low, sprawling redbrick building with its neat shrubs and swept sidewalks, the silver lettering on the wall beside the entrance. As I stepped uncertainly through the steel-and-glass doors, a smiling woman nabbed me.

"Marion," she said. "I'm Sue Henderson." Sue had graduated from Ocean Township two classes ahead of me and was now the school guidance counselor; she was responsible for my reappearance at our alma mater. She thought that as a former recipient of the Spartan Scholar award who had gone on to become an author and minor celebrity (I can hardly express how minor), I might have some advice for the honorees—things I wished I had known back when I was in their place.

Me, a role model? I seemed to recall that even back while earning academic honors, I'd come pretty close to getting kicked out of there. Then I'd gone on to blaze a trail of even more erratic behavior by a supposedly smart person, all of which I had described in print and on the air to as much of the civilized world as I could get to pay attention. Did she perhaps have me confused with some more presentable graduate?

If so, too bad. Tickled by the idea, I accepted before she could change her mind.

I hadn't realized, though, what an eerie experience coming back would be. As I entered those linoleum-and-locker-lined halls, I was swept into a crowd of kids whose faces seemed oddly familiar, though their clothes and hairstyles were a lot better than anything we used to wear. The girls in particular seemed to be ready to star in their own sitcom. With shocking instantaneousness, I was sucked back into the unbearable and constant jealousy of other people's figures that had been such a feature of teenage life for me. Apparently I had been the victim of some horrible injustice when the tiny perfect butts were handed out, and nothing had happened in the intervening decades to improve the situation.

So when Sue asked if I'd like to take a look around, I shuddered. "Oh no," I told her, "I'll just wait here." If the person I used to be and the emotions I used to feel were lurking in those halls, I wasn't eager to encounter them. Just looking at the bulletin boards, the bathrooms, the school store, and the gymnasium door from a distance was enough. I didn't want to see the ghosts: myself in the hideous blue-bloomered gym suit; myself failing the impossible quiz in chem-physics; myself with Billy Donnelly and the Garelick brothers smoking Salems in a car in the parking lot; myself finding a note from my sister in my locker saying she had run away from home with Kyle Henderson but don't tell Mommy.

High school was the only world we knew back then, the only world there was, but at least it was a captivating one, full of every kind of soap opera, rumor, and gossip, every dark secret and bright, paradoxical surface. At lunch you could find a gang of us having chocolate malts and cheeseburgers at the Towne Bite Shoppe, like nice wholesome teens. At night the scene shifted. We were out behind the Dumpster at the Y or downstairs in somebody's basement, and there wasn't a wholesome thing about it. Our class really did win the homecoming float competition four years in a row—and my pal Lou really did get sent away to a place called the Institute for Living for running a drug laboratory in his bedroom. (My mother has never forgiven me for lending him her pressure cooker.) Like little Amish girls, my sister and I spent hours and hours sewing patches on our jeans and baking giant hand-iced cookies in the shape of bunny rabbits and baskets of flowers. Unlike little Amish girls, we were usually stoned out of our minds at the time.

Just standing there in the lobby of the high school, it was all coming back to me. The dialogue in the first lesson of French 1 *("Michel? Anne? Vous travaillez?" "Euh, non, nous regardons la télévision, pourquoi?").* The modern dance moves choreographed by our assistant gym teacher Miss Dombrowski to Carly Simon's "You're So Vain." The hideous floor-length dress with lavender and white Möbius strips printed on navy polyester I wore to the junior prom, escorted by that Johnny-on-the-spot Kyle Henderson. The difference between sine, cosine, tangent, and cotangent. (Actually, no. But I did at least remember that trigonometry existed.) And then there was the night our friend Eddie Brown died driving home from a little beer party in the ASPCA parking lot.

The things that happened to me in this place were so big and so confusing I could hardly put them all together in my head. I had had the most hilarious fun and the best friends in the world, and I had also been abandoned, rejected, and desperate. I had worked hard, and I had gotten by offering as little cooperation as possible. I had been pregnant. I had been suicidal. I had been Islander #2 in *South Pacific.* I had aced the SATs and gotten suspended for smoking. I had worn out my David Bowie records, many black leotards, and seven pairs of red Converse high-tops. Then around Christmas of senior year, I had renounced it all and taken up Zen meditation.

Most of all, I had felt suffocated and wanted to GET OUT OF THERE so bad I could taste it. It seems to me now I had this feeling for most of my teens and twenties, pretty much no matter where I was. I was in a very big hurry to move along, to get on to the next thing, to escape. But as I gradually learned, most of what I wanted to escape was actually inside me, and it would be a whole lot of rushing and running later before I made peace with who I was and what I wanted out of life—before who I felt I was inside began to correspond more closely to how others perceived me. And before I found the love that was what I was really so desperate to find.

What did I know now that I wished I had known then? A fascinating question—and one I had nearly neglected to think about at all. In the way of all lifelong procrastinators, immediately after Sue called me to see if I would come back and speak, I'd forgotten about the whole thing. And it remained forgotten until the Monday before my appearance.

I was driving my friend Margaret to the airport and mentioned my upcoming, but as yet wholly unconceived, talk. She asked me what I was planning to tell them. I paused for a second.

"The path is not straight," I replied, just like that. The words hung in the air.

"That's all?" she wondered dubiously.

It turned out it wasn't. There were six more things. They came to me as if they were something I had memorized, or had been inside me all along waiting to be written down, or perhaps were being whispered by a helpful genie.

I rushed back from the airport to my computer, where I sat down and typed the seven sentences. Then the only other thing I could think of to write about them was: Duh. Isn't this what everybody already knows?

Maybe I could just, like, read a poem by Robert Frost.

Later that day, I took another look. I knew from experience that throw-it-in-the-garbage level doubt is often just a phase in the development of a perfectly good idea, and I've especially learned to have faith in things that come to me out of the blue, even if they start off looking kind of stupid and questionable. Anyway, I had to begin somewhere, and due to my procrastination, which does after all promote efficiency, this was it.

The seven things were, I realized then, some of my deepest, strongest beliefs. Though they might seem a little *Woodstock Nation*—meets—*I'm OK—You're OK,* maybe the seventies—the formative years of my worldview—had something enduring to offer after all. I mean besides aviator glasses, cheese fondue, and the Captain and Tennille singing "Muskrat Love." Back then, even the grown-ups at least pretended to believe that money wasn't everything, that you could do life your own way on your own schedule and still "make it," either by conventional standards or by your own. If you were a black sheep, if you had a nonconformist lifestyle, even if you screwed up sometimes, people loved you. Misfits were heroes; all the movies were about them.

Then Ronald Reagan got elected, John Lennon got shot, and a whole new set of ideas and accoutrements came into vogue. Everybody wanted a BMW and a job on Wall Street, then everybody wanted an IPO and a Web site, and this takes us up to last week. But I figured maybe the Spartan Scholars had heard enough about all that, about doing their best and aiming high, about how to become highly productive and supereffective achievers with Filofaxes, seven-year goals, and little ducks all in a row.

Well, I could certainly tell them something different. If I had become famous for anything it was for my mistakes, and for being absolutely candid about them in three books of memoir and on National Public Radio. But most of these episodes had come about because I was so determined to have an unconventional life; surely many of the students in the audience would feel the same way. And my view of things now was that it's often the adversity we face from within and without, the distractions that catch our eye, and the unpopular but intuitively necessary choices we make that help us become who we really are.

The seven things, I saw, were a way of talking about ambition, and self-respect, and money, and how to recover from life's surprises. They were about loneliness and frustration, decadence and diligence, commitment and impulse, and the importance of friends and family. They were about feeling different and wanting to stay that way by finding the power of one's inner weirdness, rather than seeing it as something to hide, cure, or grow out of. I had some pretty good stories to tell on this subject, I realized, both from my life and from the lives of my friends.

As I waited for my mother that night in the lobby, I saw my old history teacher Mrs. Guilford, and she said she remembered me. A good, conscientious student, she said. That was nice. Coach Dahrouge was there too—the man who taught me to drive. Or perhaps that should be "taught me to drive." Though I did ultimately get my license, I'm sure I could not be considered a driver's ed success story. The current principal, John Lysko, had been a science teacher when I was there, then known as Disco Lysko due to his long, groovy hairstyle. Everyone else I didn't know. They said Mr. Lord, the junior honors English teacher, might come, but he didn't—and they said when they'd mentioned my name to him, he'd raised his eyebrows. I think he probably remembered me a little more accurately than did Mrs. Guilford.

At that point, my mother showed up and grabbed my sons, whom I'd brought along with me. Then someone from the *Coaster,* an illustrious gazette of Jersey shore activities, was taking a picture for the paper: Sue, me, and a Spartan Scholar named Vivek Jindel. And suddenly I was onstage saying the Pledge of Allegiance, which I hardly ever say anymore.

Assistant principal Annette Caccamiso greeted the assemblage and congratulated them on their 97-or-higher grade point averages, the Spartan Scholar criterion. She read a poem by Robert Frost (close call) and then the chorus performed. Compared to the chorus when I was in it, they sounded like the Georgia Mass Choir. But I had no more time for these thoughts because Ms. Caccamiso was up there introducing me, and I was on.

I didn't know many people in the audience that night,

but as I watched their faces during the Caccamiso speech, I started to imagine I recognized a few of them. This one with the long hair and glasses was a little smarty-pants who thought she was going to win all the academic awards at graduation and then march off to Harvard. This one looked really haggard because she had just had a positive pregnancy test and couldn't tell her parents, and the boy with whom she was in love wouldn't even talk to her. This one wasn't listening because she was looking down at her thighs thinking about how fat she was and wondering how she could have been depraved enough to choose this skirt to wear tonight.

The one next to her wasn't listening either, because he had more important things to worry about, like the chemistry test and the history paper and the SATs. The one in the back in the motorcycle jacket and black jeans was a disaffected bohemian type who liked to drink and take drugs and smoke cigarettes because that was the best way to become a famous musician, and also the best way to drown out all the hideously self-conscious voices in his head. And then there was the pissed-off-looking one with the frizzy hair, her parents on either side of her, who couldn't even believe they made her come to this stupid thing, and what's worse, they were making her go to college even though she couldn't stand any school of any kind for one more goddamn minute.

All my little freaks and dreamers out there, my insomniacs and vegetarians. My poet geniuses, my mad hackers, my eggheads with dreadlocks, and my maniac brainiacs, all those Gifted and Talented and Crazy for Sures—I only hoped I knew how to talk so they would hear. Their dreams were big and strange, and their hearts were tender and breakable, and the bright shiny mass-produced moment was half blinding them to the weird and perfect futures that awaited each one just over the horizon. They were wrong about half of everything they thought they knew, but totally right about one thing. They were going Somewhere to be Somebody Someday. And if they didn't know where or who or how, this lack of certainty wasn't going to stop them from throwing themselves into the project as hard as they could.

These were my people. Like the friends I had back then and the ones I added along the way, they were the misfit musketeers who kept one another company and told one another jokes and made one another brave. And when I looked down at my paper and saw the seven things, I knew they were exactly what I had to say.

As I started to speak, I noticed that even my freaky

geniuses with better things to think about were paying attention. And afterward, after I was done and the other speeches were over, and all the kids had paraded across the stage to receive their awards, they started coming up to me and saying thank you, and their parents were hugging my mom. Everybody wanted to know if I had this thing written down somewhere.

I didn't, but now I do—though it's turned out to be kind of an extended remix. So this is for them, and for you.

the path is not straight

Let's say there's a well-lit, limited-access, four-lane high-way stretching straight and clear ahead of you, but the slow, funky back road with the doughnut shop and the cheap motels is calling your name. You call it curiosity and adventure, your parents call it stupidity and rebellion, but something in you can't resist taking the next exit.

On the other hand, let's say you have your destination firmly in mind and every intention of taking the interstate to get there—but the sawhorses are out, the orange Detour sign is up, and there's nothing you can do about it. You've taken a different road and maybe even ended up in a different place. Sometimes life rear-ends you, freezes your transmission, sticks a nail in your tire, or roars up behind you with sirens blaring and blue lights whirling—and you ain't goin' nowhere, honey, at least not for a while. Unwanted deviations from the plan are also a fact of life, and they are not always as disastrous as they first seem.

When you're young, it can seem like the routes are laid

*out, the itineraries assigned, and the outcome of the whole
stupid rat race already decided. Everybody already knows
who is pretty, who is rich, who is smart, who is a nerd with
no luck at all. Well, wait twenty years and go to your high
school reunion, as I did, and see how very wrong this is.*

*In the end, there's no rat race at all because there are
neither rats nor a race: just people, becoming who they are.*

I had planned to start my talk that night in New Jersey by
telling my audience that the path is not straight, and that
this is the thing I know now that I most wish I knew then. But
then I realized that while knowing it is a comfort, one I'm
damn glad to have when I need it, it doesn't really change
anything. No matter how many times life surprises you, it
never seems to lose its capacity to do so. Even *you* don't
lose your capacity to surprise you. Just wait till you think
you're all done and settled to see what I mean. Then wait
till the time after that. And the one after that, too.

Because the path is not straight, nor does it end every
time it seems to, life is an adventure. And as dark as the
passages and confusing as the cul-de-sacs you find yourself in, it's generally safe to assume that progress is being
made. Something is unfolding. You are becoming. But the
circuitousness of the journey is one of those things that
keep coming as a big shock.

You probably think—in fact, you can hardly be blamed for thinking—that after A and B and C comes D. That after high school comes college. That after love comes marriage, after pregnancy comes children, after hard work comes reward.

It does, but only often enough to confuse you.

The rest of the time, after A and B and C come a car accident, a job offer, a chance to run a marathon in Finland, or even just a total loss of interest in D, not to mention E and F. After high school comes the drug bust, or the pregnancy, which was supposed to come after the marriage, which instead was followed by the heartbreak or the tedium or the decision to go back to D and work in his coffee shop. Then, out of turn and when you least expect it, K and L appear on the horizon, and a couple years later you have an MBA. Or an STD.

The many derailments of life fall into two categories: the chosen and the unchosen. In chosen departures, you willfully alter your direction—often making everyone you know furious at you. They can't for the life of them understand why you chose not to take the job at the newspaper, not to start school this fall, not to marry Eric (or Erica). Instead, you are going to move to San Francisco, work on your screenplay, take a job at a ski resort, tend bar in a nightclub. Your parents are first among this group of doubters. Why? they ask. Why would you do something like this? Why do you want to mess up your whole life?

Most likely you have no good answer for them, unless you consider "Shut up and leave me alone" a good answer.

The problem is that sometimes you have *no logical information* that what you are doing is right except the feeling in your gut. It may even be true that all the logical information you have tells you to do something different. Everyone thinks you are a pigheaded fool for what you have decided, and even you start to wonder if you are, as they say, a pigheaded fool. But what you're feeling is called intuition, and you can trust it. In fact, if you don't, it spins you around and bites you really hard in the butt.

Making unpopular decisions is very difficult the first few times you try it. It's hard to stick to your guns when people you respect, or at least people you're used to letting control you, don't give you their endorsement. You feel guilty, confused, and full of doubt. Your intuition is a small voice compared to the booming unison of the pigheaded fool contingent, who by now have gotten on the horn to one another and created quite a buzz about your stupidity. And if everything doesn't go 100 percent perfectly from the moment you set out on your new path, oh, the fussing and the clucking! The warning and the wheezing! Just working themselves up to that big glorious I-told-you-so!

At first it is hard to ignore all this, but with practice it gets easier. Because in most cases you will have done the right thing and eventually they will come around to seeing that—at which point they usually start claiming they knew it all along.

These days, I can make a life-changing decision with clear conviction and hardly a peep from anyone. But I have been called a pigheaded fool many, many times. One of the most egregious was in my mid-twenties, when I decided to move to Austin, Texas, with my gay ice-skater boyfriend, later to become my first husband, rather than accept Harvard Law School's offers of admission. Boy, were my parents thrilled about that. I think they came pretty close to disowning me altogether.

And you know, I wasn't absolutely sure I was right, either. Everyone, including me for a while, had assumed I'd end up a lawyer, and be good at it. Part of me was drawn to the intense competitiveness and the intellectual challenges law school entailed. When I was next offered admission, by Boalt Hall, the law school at U.C.-Berkeley, I almost caved in. But even in Berkeley, California, the point of law school is to become a lawyer, and that was it: I didn't want to be a lawyer. I didn't want to read big books full of rules and regulations. I didn't want to file motions and study precedents. I didn't want to be deferential to judges,

I didn't want to swim through red tape, I didn't even want to dress up for work and carry a briefcase. Law school seemed exciting; practicing law did not. Even interesting, important cases with ramifications for social justice, like those I'd read about in books by F. Lee Bailey and Alan Dershowitz, seemed to involve much more caviling over details than I could ever bear.

In all the years that have passed, I have not regretted my decision. I knew I wanted something else—two things really—and I was determined to get them.

I wanted to have an unconventional life—or at the very least, I wanted to get out of the suburbs and off the fast track and see what other possibilities the world and its denizens had to offer—and I wanted even more than that to be a writer. And while it may have looked to my parents and other outsiders that I was taking every possible detour on the way to maturity, those were the two distant cities on my itinerary the whole time. They were my compasses, though many times along the journey I had to stop, regroup, and reevaluate what really was important.

What seems most unlikely to people familiar with my erratic life story is that I got to a place even my parents would recognize as success. It surprised me a little, too. Except that by that time I had started to accept the ways in which I was like my parents, so the fact that our ideas of success overlapped wasn't quite as unbelievable as it once might have been. For the path is not straight, the destination is not fixed, and the person who is taking the journey is not immutable, either.

But more on that later.

Last year my friend Justine, a bright, funny, and very beautiful girl, dropped out of college after her first semester. After all the agonizing over college admissions and choices, all the trying and waiting and hoping, not to mention paying, it had taken her less than a month to decide that she would rather be just about anywhere on earth than this place she had been dreaming of. It was a good place; it just wasn't her place, at least not then. At first her mother cried when she heard her daughter was heading off to Egypt on her own, with plans to meet friends to float down the Nile. But then she realized it wasn't the end of the world: just the Nile. She dried her tears and made Justine promise to e-mail.

One of the only reasons this didn't happen to me my first semester of college was that I barely attended it. Over Christmas of my senior year of high school, I had become obsessed with Eastern religion. I went to the library in search of books listed in the bibliography of Ram Dass's *Be Here Now;* I read Alan Watts and Aldous Huxley, Swami

Yogananda and Lao-tzu, taking copious notes in a loose-leaf binder. *Samadhi* = enlightenment! We are all one! The idea of enlightenment, of being free of mind and ego, of entering a pure state of cosmic consciousness, was very appealing to me. My mind and ego had given me nothing but problems as long as I could remember. Maybe this would be the end of the separateness that caused me so much pain.

I quit drugs and started trying to meditate. I became an official exponent of *brahmacharya,* the Sanskrit word for celibacy. I wrote away to the Lama Foundation in Taos, New Mexico, publishers of *Be Here Now,* and soon received a brochure describing summer programs at their retreat in the Sangre de Cristo Mountains. One was a two-week intensive with Ram Dass, the former Harvard professor—turned–acid guru–turned–spiritual seeker who had authored my personal bible. I begged my parents to let me go.

At seventeen, I was the youngest yogi on the mountain. Everything amazed me. The hand-built adobe buildings with mandalas carved in their wooden doors. The organic vegetarian food prepared by hippie women in long skirts. The chanting teacher Krishna Das's vats of spicy Indian tea with milk, the secret of whose deliciousness, he explained with a straight face, was that he spit in it. We meditated, we did hatha yoga, we hyperventilated in unison, we chanted to Govinda and Kali and Durga.

We weren't supposed to speak except in our private in-terviews with Ram Dass and the other teachers; rules against talking and unnecessary eye contact were sup-posed to keep the level of sexual tension under control. This didn't stop me from falling in love with Krishna Das and Sruti Ram and the rest. These guys were in their twen-ties; they had traveled in India; they had the pure faces and shining eyes and wavy hair of saints. My spiritual seek-ing was tinged with the same helpless yearning that in-formed the sex and drugs it had replaced, and I'm sure they sensed it. Nevertheless, they were very kind to me.

I started college that fall at my classy Ivy League school but my heart wasn't in it. To the bemusement of my com-puter-selected African-American roommate from Detroit, I papered my side of the dorm room with pictures of Indian gods and goddesses and their various human representa-tives. Every week, I'd skip out of school on Wednesday and hitchhike or take the bus down to New York City, where Ram Dass and his disciples were based. There were classes every day of the week, some open to the public, others by invita-tion only. I was determined to crack the hierarchy, to get into the elite sessions held on Friday and Saturday. Once I did, I was at college only two days a week.

Some of the most exclusive meetings were held at the Brooklyn home of a woman code-named Joya Santanya, a voluptuous and foulmouthed Italian housewife with snapping black eyes and thick waist-length black hair. She had been visited by the now-dead Swami Yogananda in her bathtub, had left her body for weeks, and had returned to assist Ram Dass in his teaching. She ruled the scene with an iron hand, one minute cursing and joking, the next reciting verses from the *Bhagavad Gita*.

It was Joya who dealt the blow that resulted in my departure from this rarefied realm. It happened over Christmas break, which I was spending in New York City to attend as many classes as possible, bunking in the Upper West Side apartment of Parvati, Saraswati, and Sita Om. Most of the initiates had received their Hindu names in India from their gurus, but Joya had apparently also been deputized for this purpose. You weren't supposed to ask for a name; it would be given when the time was right. Still, I hinted around when I got the chance. I thought maybe something with "Kali" in it, since I was especially fascinated by this dark, devouring incarnation of the Divine Mother with her many arms and her necklace of human skulls.

Though I had never been personally addressed by her before, something about me got Joya's attention that Christmas. She gave me my name and kicked me out in one fell swoop. "Get outta here, Tits," she said. "Go back to college and study and sleep with boys! That's what you wanna do, and that's what you should be doing."

My eyes immediately filled with tears of embarrassment and anger. "But Joya," I stammered. "I want to be with you. I want to go to God."

"Oh, come on, Tits, you can't bullshit me. I know what you want."

What could I do? Joya had spoken. In retrospect, the insight displayed by her remarks was the most convincing proof of her powers I ever saw. At the time, I was very confused and pained by what had happened. I tearfully packed up my portable *puja* table, said good-bye to Parvati and the rest, and headed back to college. I vowed to pursue my *sadhana,* my spiritual quest, on my own, and made friends around campus who shared my interests.

And then I broke my leg, and got bulimia, and became interested in Russian history, and started to hang out at the Women's Center and submit poems to the literary magazine. My life as a college student had finally gotten under way. But though some parts of the story of Marion the *yogini* are silly, the Eastern principles I absorbed and the spiritual awakening I experienced have resonated in my life to this day. They remain at the core of my understanding. Nothing else I learned that year was more important.

Justine, who floated down the Nile, went back to school too, and so did Jeff Joslin, a college friend whom I thought the coolest person on campus when I met him, our sophomore year. Shortly after we both moved into one of the cooperative group houses on campus, aka hippie central, he zoomed off into the sunset on his motorcycle. I remember waving good-bye, wishing I was going along. Instead, I inherited his copy of Jack Kerouac's *On the Road*.

Having just read that, as well as Kerouac's *The Dharma Bums,* Hermann Hesse's *Siddhartha,* Albert Camus's *The Rebel,* and Robert Pirsig's *Zen and the Art of Motorcycle Maintenance,* Jeff had decided to drop out of the Ivy League "forever." He reduced his material presence on the planet to the appropriate ascetic minimum, replacing his Stratocaster and amp with an acoustic guitar and trading his mountain parka and down sleeping bag (covered with evil, petrochemical-based nylon) for layers of wool and cotton. He and everything he carried were 100 percent biodegradable, and several times came close to proving it.

After Jeff survived some spectacularly yet predictably bad hitchhiking experiences, some near-fatal freezing nights, and a guy in a loincloth in the desert with a huge burlap sack of peyote, his departure from school turned out to be a year in length. Still, he managed to intersperse his undergraduate career and then his graduate one with VISTA volunteering, guitar playing, solar building, and garbage reclamation projects, not to mention tequila-soaked road trips to Mexico, and today he is an architect and one of the head planners for the city of Portland, Oregon.

He, too, has become something his parents could be proud of, if they were alive and/or in their right minds, which they sadly aren't. So my point is not that we persisted in our rejection of our parents' middle-class values and lifestyle. In fact, we were ultimately protected by them even while we turned our backs on them and played Derelict for a Day. Actually, the class issue is a defining one, since the whole drama of growing up is different for kids from families without money. When everything's being handed to you on a family heirloom silver platter, you can run screaming from the table and become a street person or a Hare Krishna or a drug dealer, and they'll undoubtedly save your place in case you change your mind. If there's no platter, or even no table, attaining those things rather than rejecting them is usually the issue; living on the street, selling drugs, or passing out pamphlets in the airport is far less likely to seem like an interesting lifestyle choice. (On the other hand, if you have no stake in the system, you might become much, much more serious about bringing it down.)

I'm not saying we ultimately rejected our privileges, nor is my point that we held on to every ideal we had, though we held on to a few—even after Jeff became part of the system, he remained a powerful proponent for his youthful ideals. My point is that it's okay to grow up in your way, on your own terms, on your own schedule. It's okay to take the back roads, it's okay to break the rules, and it's okay to change your mind. So if you find that the slightest divergence or resistance on your part is met with tearing of hair and gnashing of teeth and insistence that "you're throwing your life away," let me reassure you, you're not. You're just going out looking for it.

And if everyone insists that you're being "immature," remember this—it's best to get your immaturity out of the way while you're young. What's really scary is an immature forty-five-year-old.

So much for willful departures.

Sometimes it's not that you didn't have every intention of taking the main road, but it is closed. Plan B is dropped in your lap, unchosen. An accident, often literally. Someone gets hurt. Someone goes bankrupt. Someone dies. Suddenly in one second you live in a different world, one where your mother has cancer or your father is under indictment or your town has been hit by a flood. This must be how Michelle Graci, Miss New Jersey—USA 2000, felt when she was in a car accident in high school that messed up her back and scarred her face and ended her career as a gymnast, and wasn't too helpful for winning beauty contests, either. As she struggled back from this misfortune, becoming a gymnastics coach instead of a participant, she was taken into yet another stark new world when she was diagnosed with cervical cancer.

One good thing about these kinds of life-changing events is that at least no one calls you a pigheaded fool. Also, you don't have to agonize so much about what to do. Usually it is completely obvious, at least in your heart. You have to get well. You have to leave school and go home to be with your sister. You have to get a job and make some money to help your family. You have to go to rehab. You have to tell X the truth about Y. And then you have to suck up all the inspirational stories about people who managed to shine even after their lives got completely screwed up. Dedicating her reign as Miss New Jersey to breast and ovarian cancer awareness, Michelle Graci became much more than the winner of a beauty contest—she is a bona fide heroine.

If you look around, you start realizing these extraordinary people who come back from major setbacks and really lousy breaks are all over the place—from Monica Lewinsky to Lance Armstrong, from people who are responsible for their bad choices to those who have unbelievably challenging situations thrust on them through no fault of their own, to the seemingly perfect and untroubled people in the family next door. Terrifying as it is, natural and unnatural disasters are a part of life. As Harold Kushner wrote so powerfully in *When Bad Things Happen to Good People* (which I read after I got married and our first attempt to have a baby ended in a full-term stillbirth—talk about life in hell), the only power we have is to decide what kind of person we become as a result of them.

Take my friend Judy, whom I met back when we both worked at a software company in Austin, Texas. A tall redhead with a big Texas accent who was also a genius computer programmer, she was married to a writer; they lived in a really cool house and had incredible parties. Unfortunately, her enviable life dissolved one day when her husband announced out of the blue that he was leaving. Then did so, immediately and without much further discussion. For a while, she was in shock. She cried for days. Then she got really, really mad. Eventually, she quit her job and moved out of her beautiful house and did some high-paying contract programming work and a lot of country-western dancing. Judy is an incredible dancer; this and other factors resulted in a string of more or less unsuitable boyfriends. Everyone was worried. Oh God, they said, what is Judy doing with her life? Then one day she went back to school for her Ph.D., and now she is a professor of marketing at the University of Maryland and is happier than she was in the first place. That's when you know you've found your way, when you honestly feel grateful to the car that ran you off the road.

But that takes a while. I certainly did not feel pleased or grateful when I got rejected from the first two graduate schools I applied to after college. I had high GRE scores and a 4.0 GPA, I had been writing poetry since I was nine years old, and I assumed I'd have little trouble getting admitted to either the Writing Workshop at the University of Iowa or the program at Sarah Lawrence, where my idol, Grace Paley, was a teacher. Yes, these were the most prestigious MFA programs in the country, and yes, they received a hundred applications for every one they accepted, but surely one of those ones would be me. I didn't even apply anywhere else.

Well, actually, they both said no. It was quite a shock. And because it couldn't have been my grades or my test scores that they didn't like, I knew it was the poems themselves. They didn't like my writing. Which meant they didn't like me. And if they, the grand poobahs of creative writing education, the lions at the gate of my chosen career, were chasing me off, I probably should just give the whole thing up.

It was my first big capital-*f* Failure, and it was hard to take. I had already come a long way since those days in elementary school when I secretly wondered if I might be the smartest person in the whole world. By the time I got to college, I had realized I wasn't even the smartest person in the building, or on any one floor. I thought I was widely read, had a gift for languages, was a bit of a math whiz. Well, in each of these areas, there were people around who made me look mentally handicapped. But though I had come to have a more humble and realistic view of my capabilities and how they compared to other people's, I still had plenty of ego left. And writing was one area where I was sure I had something special. At least before those brief letters of rejection stated so clearly otherwise.

So, what to do? First, I had to understand what had happened somehow—make up some reasonable explanation that wasn't simply "Because you suck," so I would have somewhere to go with it in my head. This process is often dismissively described as rationalization or making excuses, but it is really part of recovering from failure and planning a next step. Here's what I came up with. As an undergraduate I had had trouble getting into the writing workshops I wanted to take. The explanation I heard was that my style was too pop, too anti-intellectual, too influenced by rock lyrics. I figured that this might be the case again. And I thought, Okay, fine. I'll go into advertising. Those flaws would be assets there.

Since I had absolutely no background in the field, I signed up for a couple of semesters of undergraduate classes in advertising at the University of Texas (I was by this time living in Austin) in preparation for applying to their master's program. And in fact I had a great time in these classes and excelled at the work. My writing *was* perfect for advertising, and I enjoyed the artistic and practical aspects of it as well.

But as well suited as my skills might have been, my heart wasn't in it. You can't go straight from being a Marxist-Leninist-feminist revolutionary, as I saw myself in college, to being a shill for frozen dinners and compact cars without some kind of major ideological overhaul, and it just wasn't happening. I kept looking longingly at the classes in the English department. The graduate poetry workshops. The seminars in women's literature. I got permission from the professors to enroll in these classes, and before I knew it, I had a year of course work toward an MFA without ever having been accepted into a program.

When I applied to schools a second time, I aimed less high, though I still looked for a place with teachers with whom I wanted to study. I ended up at Brooklyn College, in New York City, because John Ashbery, a poet I much admired, was there. We got along so poorly that I had to transfer to the fiction department. Where, wonder of wonders, the professors really liked my writing. Later on, at the software company, I used all my advertising skills, and in the end I even got to study with Grace Paley, at a summer workshop in Oregon. And that lowbrow writing style of mine has worked out pretty well after all, so I'm glad I didn't go off and learn to write like a real smart person.

Thank you, Iowa; thank you, Sarah Lawrence; thank you, John Ashbery; and while we're at it, thank you, Judy's ex-husband. It's an odd truth that the people and institutions who reject us and screw up our plans often give us a gift neither they nor we can see.

If you think high school is the place where your whole life gets decided, think again. This became very clear to me when I attended my twentieth high school reunion. By the time I went to this shindig, in 1995, held not in the high

school itself but in the ballroom of a nearby hotel in subur-
ban New Jersey, I thought I was really returning in triumph.
Look, it's Marion Winik! I could imagine them whispering.
Can you believe what a famous and beautiful celebrity she
turned out to be? Have you read her books? Did you see her
on the *Today* show? Is it true she's been in *People* magazine?

Well, the problem with the people I went to high school
with is that they're the people I went to high school with.
Everyone talked during the speeches (including mine, I'm
sorry to say). Nobody ate their green beans. And in most
cases, the girls had to ask the boys to dance. The old love
affairs seemed to retain a little heat, the ancient cliques
almost managed to re-form, and if a bell had rung, I'm
sure the entire assemblage would have marched out of
there and looked for the next class.

Though group behavior hadn't evolved much in two
decades, physical appearance was another story; in some
cases, connecting the name on the name tag to the person
it was stuck to was a virtually psychedelic experience.
Tommy Vignola?!? Wanda Williams! Fred Wood! After a
while, I noticed that *V*s and *W*s, my old homeroom companions, were the names that evoked the most intense nostal-
gia. After all those years of roll call, you can't help but
remember your part of the alphabet best.

In general, the men looked much worse at thirty-eight than they had as slender youths of eighteen with hair, while the women, ha ha, looked the same or better. (In another twenty years, I fear the tables may be turned again.) Decked out in a red Stetson and cowboy boots, I fell into the late-bloomer category, as noted by the classmate who I'm sure thought she was paying me a compliment when she charged up to me at the bar and said, "If there's a vote for the most changed person, I'm voting for you! You look excellent!"

Perhaps because of the democratizing effects of middle age on the body, people were far less threatening than they once had been. One friend noted that while the class as a whole probably had the same total weight, it certainly was distributed differently. And life has not turned out to be the ruthless popularity contest it once was, with such narrowly defined parameters of success. The football players are just big guys now and the cheerleaders drive car pools like everybody else, while many of the social outcasts and oddball geniuses have grown up into the people they were secretly plotting to be.

Except for the honors student—turned—TV weatherman, who may have finally gotten the attention of the runner-up for homecoming queen, there seemed to be no plans for an after party. Nope, the wild all-nighter, held after the prom, after graduation, even after the ten-year reunion, is a thing of the past. Maybe it's just too easy: no basements to sneak into, no parents to hide from, no fake ID, no tests to take in the morning. No matter how many doobies we smoked at how many rock concerts in the seventies, it was clear that we now own landscaping businesses and wear our seat belts. We are the parents, and the basements are our own. When I tell you how unlikely this once would have seemed . . . well, just as unlikely as adulthood seems to you now.

Finally, as the open bar closed, all was forgiven. Broken hearts, lost student council elections, even practical jokes played in study halls years ago. Even one erstwhile boyfriend's wife seemed to have gotten over the detailed description of my high school love affair with her husband I had recently given in an article for *Cosmo,* "A Nymphomaniac Grows Up." And though some of the former cheerleaders seemed to be as condescending as ever, I started to realize this might be my attitude problem, not theirs.

I was sitting outside on a planter with former archrival, valedictorian, and ballerina Dr. Robin Altman herself, hugging and crying because at last, it didn't matter which one of us was smarter. (Maybe it never mattered in the first place.) The pecking order was dissolved, the organic whole diffused. We no longer belonged to each other.

So the doctor and I sat there and watched the farewell hugs dissolve and the kisses blow away, the reunited disassemble and straggle off to their cars and back to their separate worlds.

Can you believe it? We actually did go out and get a life, after all.

mistakes need not be fatal

One thing that is certain as you move ahead in life is that you will make mistakes—little teeny mistakes; somewhat bigger, messier mistakes; and huge, horrific, hellish mistakes that take years to deal with. Personally I am responsible for a vast panoply of mistakes of all sizes and varieties. But since I've devoted three books to them already, and you can explore the Winik Oeuvre de Boo-boo in depth as you see fit, I will only recap some of the highlights here.

In any case, there would be little point in doing otherwise, since even if someone had suggested to me way back when how badly some of my decisions would turn out—and come to think of it, they probably did—I think I would have made the mistakes anyway. Cautionary tales just don't work. While it is comforting, fascinating, and often hilarious to hear about other people's screwups and the consequences they suffered as a result, it does not seem to stop us from enacting them ourselves, especially if we are the unruly type. We learn from our own lived experience, not the experiences of others. So the focus here will not be on trying to get you to eschew mistakes but on what to do once you've made them. Stops along the way include

- *the seven deadly sins and you*
- *mistakes can be teachers*
- *how to deal with shame*
- *okay, one little mistake story*
- *drugs and alcohol—the actual reason why they suck*
- *secrets of bouncing back*
- *a little story about my first winter in Pennsylvania*
- *the Ph.D. who was expelled from high school*

I was never a careful person and I took many risks. It is no exaggeration to say I am lucky to be alive. A lot of people I know, or knew, are not. Drugs and AIDS took a particularly brutal toll on my generation, not to mention my closest circle of friends and immediate family (one husband and two brothers-in-law, to be exact—I thought of writing "so far" but I couldn't bear to). The chances I took as a young person involved me in situations ranging from teen pregnancy to IV drug abuse to various illegal pranks that seemed at the time to be "revolutionary activities."

I am not saying it is a good idea to do these things, but I am saying you can come back from almost anywhere. You haven't made a fatal mistake until you are actually dead. And the mistakes that don't kill you teach you unforgettable lessons. Big mistakes—the ones that lead to deaths, addictions, crimes, car accidents, prison, and other personal disasters and tragedies—are the toughest teachers, with the lessons that hurt to learn, the ones that force you to change the way you think and live. But little mistakes teach too. Like telling a lie to a friend. Telling a lie to almost anyone, for that matter. Being thoughtless, inconsiderate, or needlessly harsh with someone. Making a lazy choice or an easy choice instead of what you know is the right choice. Even at my advanced age, I continue to make judgment errors in both my business and personal life, never with evil intentions, often with a kind of oh-it'll-be-all-right carelessness, and I have found that even little sins of omission can have quite a kickback.

Speaking of sins, I remember doing a jigsaw puzzle when I was a child, called "The Seven Deadly Sins." (Okay, so my moral education was a bit catch-as-catch-can.) The puzzle had pictures of some Caligula-type dude in various vignettes depicting the big seven: pride, envy, greed, sloth, gluttony, lust, and anger. I remember being fascinated by these images and this whole idea. I wondered if I would get to do any of them when I grew up.

Little did I know that some days would be jam-packed with all seven, and that far from being deadly, they would instead leave me alive and squirming with regret and shame. Sometimes dead seemed like the easy way out, really. But if they weren't fatal, they certainly were hard to avoid. Though I don't attribute the problem to an incident with a snake and an apple, I have come to believe the so-called sins are innate, germinating in our personalities from babyhood. Unless you are planning to spend the rest of your life in a monastery, your associates and the media will actually incite and encourage them; even in the monastery, you can expect to struggle with them on a regular basis.

You will feel lust, and greed, and envy. You will pig out, you will seethe with rage, you will lie abed and think how very fine you are. In my view, all of this is natural and blameless, and in fact some of these impulses will be responsible for your best actions in life. It is lust that got me married to such a delectable husband, greed and envy that sit me down at this computer every day, and gluttony that drives me deep into the pages of *The Joy of Cooking* to emerge with a sour cherry pie. God, that was a good pie.

The vices, and I think they are better called vices than sins, can be both useful and even somewhat adorable, if kept under control. Your task, in fact, will be to do just that, as if you were a dog walker and these were your seven unruly charges. Every day you make it back to the house with both the rottweiler of rage and the Lhasa apso of lust still on the leash will be a big achievement. But some days, one of the dogs gets loose and wreaks havoc in the park. The poodle of pride sinks his teeth into your leg, the beagle of sloth wee-wees on your handbag, and the yapping Chihuahua of envy destroys all your close relationships. This is what we are calling here a "mistake."

Example: You steal a twenty out of your mother's purse or do something dishonest at work.

Example: You kiss someone besides the person who has every right to think he or she is your one and only. Or you kiss someone else's one and only—like, say, your sister's boyfriend.

Example: You break the confidence of a friend, thus allying with a third person against her.

Example: You take something from a store.

Example: You take credit for something you didn't do.

Example: You drink too much or take too many drugs or both, and then proceed to get in your car and drive, or have sex with someone you wouldn't have had sex with otherwise, or make stupid, hurtful comments to a classmate, or perhaps put on some kind of really humiliating performance at a party—say, stripping to your underwear, getting in the swimming pool, and giving a poetry recital, then screaming that your watch is lost, insisting that everyone scour the pool and the grounds looking for it for an hour before you then find it in your pocket (at which point, no one can believe it is a ten-dollar Timex).

I mention these only because I've been guilty of every one of them. And I know how the feeling of shame can fill you up like poison, like pollution in your head, until you feel so bad you can hardly recognize yourself in there. And don't really want to, either. The sense of doom that follows these mistakes—now I've done it, now I'm screwed, now everything is ruined—is one that you can hardly help but experience when you bring disaster down on your own head. You feel trapped, desperate, even slimy. The very worst is when you've compromised your integrity—which basically just means you've done something you yourself don't approve of, something that goes against your own idea of who you are and what you would and wouldn't do. This poetry reading thing may not sound so bad to you, but the last time I did it was the last time I drank. I was forty, and I just couldn't take being that much of a public idiot anymore.

Shame has its place in life: it's the wake-up call that puts an end to the long, confused night of misbehavior, that drags you out in the cold yellow morning, shivering, wrong, and alone. But too much shame for too long is counterproductive. You cannot get better, mired in guilt and self-abnegation. You can't move on and start acting the way you'd like while feeling unworthy and hopeless.

One of the contributions of Dr. Bruno Bettelheim, a famous child-rearing expert, is that good relations between parent and child are dependent on a "lenient response" to the imperfections of both oneself and one's child. Well, this is true in dealing with yourself, too. You are only human. You fucked up. But all the time you spend brooding and punishing yourself is more time when your best self still cannot emerge. Being depressed is not all that much better than being bad, at least from the point of view of getting on with your life in a positive, productive way.

I have found that the best thing to do when you're feeling this way, or at least the first step, is to talk about what happened. If you can own up to your mistakes, if you can speak them, hear them, and accept them, you'll find that they stop poisoning you and making you sick. Some people spend their whole life trying to cover up the blundering and stumbling in their past, trying to run from whoever they used to be. But I think you can make your mistakes a part of who you are in a positive way. Then they become part of your strength, part of your arsenal, part of your wisdom, and a connection between you and other people—rather than a closed door you can't let anyone open, ever.

If you're an artist, your mistakes will feed your art. If you work with people, they will feed your understanding. And no matter what you do, the mistakes you live with enrich your humanity, your understanding of life's dark and bitter possibilities, and your respect for both virtue and good fortune.

My student Nicole started her freshman year of college with no money except for the small amount Mom and Dad would deposit in her savings account each month. Such a babe in the woods was she financially, she didn't even have a checkbook. Then guess what showed up in her mailbox? Her very own shiny new credit card! Her mom sternly advised her never to use it unless she absolutely needed to. Well, of course, since she would have no way to pay the bills, she agreed. But quickly her idea of really needing something expanded from a car emergency to that cute shirt at the Gap. She was charging snacks, concert tickets, gas. She thought that she would pay it all off by the end of the summer. Right. By junior year, she had accrued two more cards and $4,000 debt.

She didn't know what to do; she was afraid to tell her

parents or anyone else. Worry dogged her day and night. Then she read the story of a Texas college student who had committed suicide under the pressure of credit card debt not all that much greater than hers. So instead of keeping it all inside, she started to talk to people. Soon she realized she was far from alone: due to the intensive marketing practices of the credit card companies on college campuses, there were many, many students in the same boat. In fact, as she later learned, there was legislation to stop these practices pending in Washington.

In the magazine writing class she took with me her senior year, Nicole decided to write a piece on this subject. The essay included her personal experience, the experiences of others, and the advice she had gathered about how to handle the situation. The discussion of her work in class was one of the more spirited we had that semester, and the humiliation she had so dreaded simply wasn't there.

Talking and writing and connecting with others didn't make the debt go away. But it was the antidote for the shame that can literally kill you.

The story has another, even happier ending: the article she wrote helped her land her first job in journalism after college. So she finally has some money to send the credit card company!

• • •

I've mentioned drugs and lying and major debt, yet the mistake that brings you shame doesn't even have to be that serious. It can be a tiny little moment of carelessness, like the time I backed out of my mother's garage a bit too breezily and ripped the right outside mirror off her brand new white Nissan Maxima. (I don't know about you, but I have had quite a long run of bad karma with such mirrors.) I stood in the driveway with the mirror in my hand, which was still hanging by a wire or two, trying to stuff the whole business back into the hole, furious with myself and so depressed about having to tell my mother, who was in the house feeling all jolly about her fancy new car. As I always do in these situations, I tried to think how much worse it could have been. I could have smashed the whole side of the thing. I could have run over the dog or plowed through the rock garden. Despite these encouraging thoughts, I still felt like an incorrigible idiot. I just wanted to smack myself.

I often have this feeling. For example, not long ago, I was going through a tense period with my husband, Crispin. One night during this time, he was sitting at his desk reading his e-mail when I came up from behind him to ask a question. He immediately clicked the close box on the message he was reading and swiveled around to answer me. But something in that click and swivel piqued my curiosity. What was he reading that he had to close so fast?

Well, I stewed about this for the rest of the evening until he went upstairs to read the boys a bedtime story. And then I went to his computer, got into the e-mail program, and looked at the incoming messages. There was one from a close female friend and confidante of his who lives far away but with whom he e-mails quite frequently. I can't say I paused for a moment's reconsideration before I opened it up and started to read. I quickly gathered that he had been writing to her about our problems and she was responding with her analysis, which was that I was "filled with self-loathing" and would do anything to make him reject me in order to fulfill my self-destructive expectations. She went on to offer her condolences for what she foresaw might be a second failed marriage—she could hardly bear to see him go through it, she knew how devastating it would be.

What??? First of all, we had been married less than six months and intimations of our demise were premature, to say the least. Second, she didn't even *know* me, having met me once at our wedding, though I suppose she could claim to have deduced her insights into my personality from reading my books. But, third, it wasn't even true. Maybe a long time ago—maybe. But nowadays I reserve my loathing for the truly deserving, and believe me, I did not move myself and my household two thousand miles across the country to see if I could get my blue-eyed beloved to reject me. And fourth, *she* must be in love with him herself and was just trying to speed up his getting rid of me so she could get back his undivided attention, could have him writing her e-mails three times a day as he did before we were married.

But fifth, I had snooped into his e-mail and read his private correspondence, so how could I even talk to him about it? I was so upset by what I'd read and what I'd done, and by the idea that he might be taking her counsel to heart, that I was on the verge of tears. I moped silently around the house for a while, then lay on my bed in the dark, alternately tossing and turning and staring into space. It seemed like my invasion of his privacy was actually the most wrong act committed in the situation—after all, it wasn't wrong for him to ask her opinion, and it wasn't wrong for her to give it (though the opinion itself was way, way wrong). What was undeniably and inexcusably wrong was to read somebody else's e-mail. I was so embarrassed and ashamed that even being the pathological confessor that I am, I couldn't imagine how to tell him about it.

And then he walked into the bedroom and said, "What in God's name is the matter with you? You're acting like your best friend died."

And then, because I really do know better than to compound a mistake with a festering secret, I spilled the whole story. And at that very moment it started to get better. While he wasn't thrilled that I had read his e-mail, he could well understand why I was so upset and was much more concerned with assuring me that he knew his pen pal was totally off base than with being angry at me.

You can't be forgiven until you confess, and this is true even with forgiving yourself. When you start talking about it, you start accepting. When you start accepting, you start forgiving. And then you can start the real work: bouncing back.

How do you bounce back? You clean up your mess, if possible, and apologize, if possible. And you study the situation to see what you can learn. And you take big, deep breaths of fresh air. And you do something good or kind or hard or right to balance it out, and get back to the place where you like yourself again.

Bouncing back from the rearview mirror incident, or from my adventures in e-mail espionage, took a couple of days. On the other hand, I think I've been bouncing back from my adventures with drugs and alcohol almost continually since they happened. For one thing, it took me a while to learn the basic lesson, which was, Okay, stop now, for real. And then I had to figure out what it all meant. What it meant that I used drugs in the first place, that I liked it at the time, that other people paid with their lives and I did not, that other people who followed the same basic path as I have come to different conclusions—that, for example, they go to twelve-step meetings and I don't. Maybe that's because some part of me still admires party attitude—abandon, excess, even decadence. Maybe that means I'm not at the end of the road yet.

A lot of people my age smoked pot in high school—back then, even some of the adults were trying pot. But a much smaller group felt compelled to ingest every drug that was available, as I was seemingly committed to do, and fewer still got to the place where I was in my early twenties—an Ivy League graduate working on her master's degree, with a full-time job developing study materials for the LSAT, while shooting heroin and cocaine almost every day.

Sound like fun? Well, it was, actually, sometimes, hanging out with my housemates in our fifth-floor New York apartment blasting the Pointer Sisters and partying like it was 1999. Of course, if it had been no fun at all, we would never have been so gung ho about it. I think it's a blind spot of most antidrug efforts to refuse to admit that one of the reasons people do drugs is that at least some of the time, they have a good time. But it is also true that once you have those good times, you try to keep having them. And then bad things start happening. For me, the bad things included passing out with a needle in my arm, getting beaten up and ripped off trying to cop, seeming so messed up at work that my boss escorted me home on the subway one night and pleaded with me to slow down. Worst of all, having a boyfriend I was quite in love with break up with me because he just couldn't handle the craziness of me and my world.

After that shattering experience, it was hardly any fun at all, but like most people who go this far, I was now too caught up in trying to re-create my old good drug experiences to stop. This, finally, is the worst thing about drugs: not only are the drug experiences themselves eventually pleasureless, but they also rob all the joy from ordinary experience, so that you end up being jealous of everyone in the world, even just people you see closing their garage doors as you drive down the street. Oh God, you think, if only I could be just an ordinary person, closing my garage door. How innocent and lucky they are, that they can just do a simple thing like that and have it be what it is and nothing more. For you, it would be either that you were high while closing the door or that you weren't high and wanted to be. The high / not-high dichotomy swallows up the door-closing experience as well as every other one in your life: birthday parties, weddings, work, sex, listening to music, going to sleep, job interviews, getting together with friends, falling in love, even dying. Nothing is itself anymore.

Nineteen eighty-two was a very bad year for me, and 1983 could have been my last, I think, if my life hadn't taken a surprising turn involving a gay figure-skating bartender at Mardi Gras in New Orleans. Which certainly didn't lead immediately to sobriety, but at least it gave me some reason to wake up the next morning.

Whenever I tell this story, people always want to know how it is that I didn't become chemically dependent on drugs and have to go into treatment, didn't lose my job, didn't die of an overdose. How can that possibly be? Well, first of all, I think it's tempting to mistake what was mostly just outlandish and undeserved good fortune for something else. Mainly I was just unbelievably lucky. And why didn't I get AIDS when so many around me did? I cannot tell you, except to acknowledge that same lifesaving luck. Since my partying days came in the early eighties, before the virus even had a name and before we knew it was so important not to share needles, it really is a miracle that I am not dead. I did get hepatitis C, though, and that's another reason why I don't drink anymore.

If there is anything else, any lifesaving quality of mine, I'd say it's this: however predisposed I was to party my brains out, I was also an ambitious creature with big plans. As much as I loved to get high, I was not going to totally fuck up my life. I was about one iota less self-destructive than that. Every time I hit the downside of the drug roller-coaster, my guilt, my sense of responsibility, and my grandiose self-concept would kick in, creating an internal limit that stopped me short of shooting up every single day, burning my bridges, or exhausting my resources. It's as if I had two basic urges: to be both as bad and as good as I could be. To succeed and achieve, and to rebel and fuck up. For a long time neither one truly had the upper hand, and I was lucky enough to live long enough to realize that actually neither one of them is the most important thing for me.

What is the most important thing for me is love. And the experience of love that finally straightened me out was having kids. The overwhelming miracle of having and nurturing babies changed my life and my head more than any drug ever could. My idea of acceptable risk began to diminish, and my attachment to wholesome and life-giving pursuits simultaneously zoomed. Though my appetite for altered states has never fully left me, nowadays I have too many people to take care of. Even bungee jumping, which I did a few short years ago, seems stupid to me now. I think I'm left with sex and running (who knew that exercise produced such a head rush?) and playing my favorite songs really, really loud.

As a mother, I hope and pray that my kids are not as crazy as I was, and that they're nearly as lucky. I feel I will get nowhere by lying to them, by refusing to share what I know of both the appeal and the risk of drugs. I'm still sorting it all out, and though I'm nobody's role model, I have a lot of stories that they might want to hear. My inability to be completely black-and-white on this issue is either a fatal flaw or a saving grace—I guess we won't know until the final results are in.

Sometimes it's up to you just how fatal a mistake has to be. My friend and former boss Morgan Jones was the veteran of many risky decisions and flying leaps, and somehow he'd always made it to the other side of the abyss. But recently he found himself at the very bottom.

At the age of forty-two, having worked like a madman since he was fifteen years old, Morgan sold that software company Judy and I worked for, one he'd built from scratch, for $2.5 million and stock options. Two buyouts later, his options became IBM stock and Morgan was truly a wealthy man.

He had always said he was going to retire by forty-five, and he did. From being a crazed workaholic with cross-addictions to both milk shakes and Mexican beer, he transformed himself into a triathlete and a macrobiotic health nut, pouring the same energy into those new pursuits as he had into the building of his company. Then, at his macro hangout, he met a beautiful dancer / cross-country bicyclist half his age. He fell madly in love and got engaged. However, his young girlfriend was uncertain about marriage; she broke their engagement and went home to Montana to reconsider. One afternoon in a van on a frozen road, she was in a horrible accident. The doctors said she would never walk again.

Morgan rushed to her side, determined to override this prognosis by sheer will if necessary. Those who knew him did not doubt it was possible.

Over the next two years, Morgan spent a substantial portion of his fortune on his love's rehabilitation, while she poured in every ounce of discipline, faith, and determination she had. He took her all over for therapy, remodeled houses for her convenience, located tropical resorts for the handicapped, found even-more-advanced rehab programs—and it actually worked, to some extent. She re-covered capabilities far beyond what the doctors had pre-dicted and could even walk with braces.

As his spending increased, Morgan became worried that his cash reserves might not be enough. He began investing in the stock market, then day trading on-line in earnest. The adrenaline rush was addictive—he was gaining, or some-times losing, as much as $300,000 a day. Though at first he made enough to cover their expenses, eventually his losses started to build. Meanwhile, his girlfriend was craving a quieter life, one in which Morgan was not on the computer and watching CNBC all day. So they moved to Oahu, and he gave his last $200,000 to a bond trader to handle.

Then something happened that Morgan really didn't see coming. It turns out that even in a wheelchair, you can run off with another man. Well, as you'll recall, leaving him was what she was doing when she had the accident in the first place.

In a depression blacker than any he had ever known, Morgan decided to commit suicide. He sounded serious enough that a good friend from Seattle flew down as soon as she got off the phone with him. She made Morgan an offer. If he would wait six months, she would give him a foolproof herbal cocktail that would kill him painlessly. He agreed to the plan.

He spent the next six months writing letters of apology to all the women he had mistreated in his life, since he finally knew what it felt like. Meanwhile, his bond trader had a run of bad luck and lost all of Morgan's money and more, buying on margin. Well, this was good news, actually. It meant he would have to get a job. He passed up the cocktail, returned to Austin, and started looking. Soon he was back in the thick of the high-tech industry, working on a secret project relating to the Internet. He's hooked up with the crazy smart people he loves and is dating several eligible bachelorettes. When I talked to him the other day, he said he's the happiest he has ever been.

Like all the best mistakes, Morgan's folly has become a lesson: the biggest and most emotionally costly lesson of his life. It has taught him the value of complete honesty, stripped him of the fear of having no money, and shown him that pain and despair can be the wisest teachers. He can laugh when he tells this story, but only because he's already shed the tears.

Being a writer, and a reader, has certainly helped me see that mistakes are part of just about every interesting tale. Look at any novel or memoir—the characters tumble down into darkness, then struggle back into the light. It's the way the story goes. So right after I do whatever incredibly stupid thing I have gone and done, or a few months into the big new project or life choice that's not working out, my mind starts picking out the narrative line. And finding the humor. <u>Because once you can laugh, you can move on.</u>

A sense of story and sense of humor: these are not quite like the *GET OUT OF JAIL FREE* card in Monopoly, but they will make your prison sentence much shorter and easier to bear. This is why people tell funny stories at funerals and make jokes about diseases and disasters, and in fact it's a big part of why people talk at all. When I recently moved across the country and lost the daily contact with friends that had been a part of life I took totally for granted, I found my problems seemed much more terrible and my dark moods much more impenetrable than they ever had. Then a few of my old buddies came to visit me, and within hours we were all upstairs, lying on my big bed, and I was telling them the story of my trials and tribulations, and there were sad parts and funny parts, and I went on and on, and even though they all were just about asleep when I finished, I felt radically, breathtakingly better.

And you know, I think I might feel better still if I told it one more time.

I had quite a first winter in the Pennsylvania country-side, having moved here after living in Texas for twenty years. The snow situation was baroque: high winds blew the powder across the cornfields into our quarter-mile-long hilly driveway, drifting it into mini mountains. This same wind also whipped the trampoline into the woods and wrapped it around a tree, and smashed the glass top of a patio table. Jesse Garver and his front-loader (no mere snowplow would do) had to come dig us out three times a week, at sixty bucks an hour. One day when the driveway was clogged I was trying to four-wheel across the fields in our Dodge Durango—the Honda had been an ice sculpture for weeks—and I drove the car into a snow-covered creek. The entire rear end was four feet up in the air.

We heat with wood—so, of course, the chimney clogged, which we found out when the house filled with smoke. The guy we buy wood from unclogged it by firing sixteen rifle shots down it, first with a pistol, then with a rifle. He came out with his face pitch black, temporarily deaf in one ear.

Right about that time, my husband fell down the stairs while putting away Christmas decorations and broke his foot. He had to hike up the snowy driveway on crutches several times and was completely off woodstove duty. Then Justine brought me her cat to take care of while she floated down the Nile, and it immediately disappeared. All family members searched the house and surrounding area for days. Then it snowed again and we figured we might as well stop looking.

The well pump broke in a blizzard in the middle of the Super Bowl, which meant not only were we stuck in the house, but we had no water, and even if a plumber would have come during the Super Bowl, there was no way to get up the driveway. Soon after the water was fixed the following week, the basement flooded because I had accidentally left on an outside faucet when the pump was broken, and it ran and ran until it soaked through the whole house into the basement.

In the process of cleaning up the two hundred gallons of water and wet furniture, I found the cat. It wasn't dead, but it was smelly and skinny and filthy and sick, and its fangs had grown down past its chin. After a week of feeding it vitamins by hand and trying to clean it off and cheer it up, it died the second I walked in the door of the vet. Despite my protests, the vet did some kind of Code Blue procedure to revive it, which did not work but cost a lot of money. And I'm not even going to go into the problems I was having with my husband, which you might guess from the little e-mail episode I mentioned.

For some reason my friends were laughing hysterically when I told them all of this, and soon I was laughing too. What I needed was to make my little raft of troubles into a story, and I needed to tell it. In fact, sometimes I need to tell it about twelve or thirteen times. It's tough, I know, but that's why we have friends. And psychiatrists.

This husband of mine, who is a Ph.D. in philosophy and a college professor, is still telling the story of how he got expelled from high school. A highly political and very angry adolescent, he idolized Che Guevara and Malcolm X. He thought of himself as a dangerous revolutionary. It was his mission to disrupt the operation of the school system, which he saw as a mindless prison run by bureaucrats; he self-published a school newsletter regularly denouncing it in just those terms. He set off a stink bomb in the hall that had the building reeking for years, and tried every way he could to shut the place down. Perhaps he got some of these ideas from his favorite book at the time—*The Student As Nigger.*

As you can imagine, by the time he got to high school, he had been in trouble at school on many occasions. So when he ran for the student government on the platform of dissolving the student government and grabbed the microphone in the middle of an assembly to shout his battle cry, the authorities decided not to wait around. They expelled him.

Crispin believes now that getting expelled from school

may have been the best thing for him. At least it saved him from committing further subversive actions that might have endangered himself and others. At the alternative hippie school where he enrolled instead, he was surrounded by like-minded people. He could stop fighting so hard, and even start learning again. By senior year, he was ready to apply to college. And because he loved books and ideas as much as he hated stupid rules and bureaucracies, he has pretty much stayed there for the rest of his life.

people are more important
than achievements or possessions

3

This is actually something you already know perfectly well, but you risk forgetting it as you grow up. Not to say that you won't continue to parrot it earnestly; most everyone does, even if their behavior says, Bye, honey, I'll be driving off to work in the Jaguar now. It can be gradually drummed out of you by our culture's emphasis on doing and getting or by the incredible risks and pain sometimes involved in connecting. For example, when Crispin the Hermit Boy saw this piece of advice on my list, he scoffed that the better suggestion would be, "People come and go—buy a good stereo."

Well, you know, a good stereo is a fine thing, too. So I will talk about all three of these pursuits—connecting, accomplishing, and acquiring—and the ways they balance our lives.

When I was planning my speech for the Spartan Scholars, I wanted to make sure I talked about the most important

thing I took with me from high school. It was not my knowledge of calculus (long forgotten), or my favorite denim
skirt (long unraveled), or even my old love letters (though
these I still have in a Chinese tea tin in a drawer in my
old bedroom at my mother's house). I knew without a
moment's thought that the most important thing was my
friendship with Sandye.

Sandye and I met the year we were both eight, when her
family moved into the house at 64 Dwight Drive, down the
street from us, at number 7. The ends of our long street
were like whole different worlds to me then. Hers had a
group of big, intimidating boys (probably all of eleven or
twelve years old) who seemed like an urban gang compared
to our scrape-kneed bunch of brats; once they threw eggs
at us on Halloween. Yet I would gladly brave this and any
other hazards along the way when invited to come up and
play in her pink-and-purple bedroom. Her mother was a
health nut, which was very unusual back then. Everyone in
the family took vitamins and supplements and honey-
colored wheat germ caps from a divided plastic tray; when
I was over I was allowed to take them, too.

Our friendship was cemented in the undertaking of our
first big joint project in fifth grade. We put on a show depicting all the members of our class, using homemade sock
puppets with tennis balls stuck inside them. We believed

this to be a hilarious satire (those portrayed perhaps did not) and gaily reprised it the next year. In seventh, our rock opera version of Shakespeare's *Julius Caesar* was virtually a Broadway hit. I still find myself singing our lyrics, three decades later, to the tunes we borrowed from the Beatles and *Jesus Christ Superstar*.

High school is when this sisterhood came into its own; having survived those four years together, we were closer than ever. I remember carrying Sandye around on my shoulders through the halls one Friday afternoon of senior year, both of us singing Van Morrison's "Moondance." (I wasn't that much bigger than she but I was always a macho show-off, ripping caps off bottles with my teeth or diving into the gray Atlantic in the winter.) At that age, at that time, our friendship felt like magic.

Yet the road of our friendship had its bumps. Even in fifth grade, Sandye had a group of other friends that I wasn't part of, and they had a little newsletter that they passed around, with comics depicting people as all hair with feet sticking out, like Cousin Itt on *The Addams Family*. I believed back then that it was devoted to making fun of me. Actually I believed this until pretty recently, but Sandye has always insisted that it's not true. I was a rather insecure and jealous person in seventh grade, and I focused a lot of this on Sandye, and when the boy I liked liked her better (this happened at least half a dozen times over the years), it didn't help. There I was like a character in some French play, wisely counseling the young Monsieur M___ about how to get Sandye's attention, while it was me who really cared. *Merde.*

The summer after our freshman year of college, we went to Europe. Sandye had already dropped out of Brandeis, where she'd been on a full scholarship, because it was mostly too much like high school. Unbelievably enough, her father had won a red TR-6 convertible in a contest and had arranged for us to pick it up in London. I was still a little on the holy side from my bout with spiritual seeking, but the trip proved to be just the thing. Sandye had me guzzling red wine out of the bottle by the time we were on the ferry to Calais.

Outside Paris, a man ran into the road shouting, "Pull over, pull over, the Tour de France is coming through!" In the excitement of the moment, Sandye veered into a ditch and flipped the car. We were trapped there, unhurt but upside down and a little hysterical, while bicycles whizzed by and cyclists laughed down at us for a half hour. When they were gone, we emerged from the car like heroic aviators, and the residents of Chevreuse turned their attention to the plight of our vehicle. After some extremely skillful moves with a tractor, it was on the street, upright, with hardly a scratch. We had to stay and celebrate, of course.

With her dark curls, cat green eyes, and curvy figure, Sandye was a raging success with the men of the Old World. She and the Chevreuse postman were a hot item; we stayed in the village for two days and went out only for crepes and cider. I was an essential part of the picture because Sandye did not speak French and I did. *(Michel! Anne! Vous travaillez?)* My celibacy was all I had left of my spiritual quest, though at this point its only real purpose was to save me from having to compete with Sandye.

In Luzern, Switzerland, I finally got a little enlightenment. A couple of local guys bought us beers at the rathskeller, then invited us back to their apartment. It was a very nice apartment, full of shag-rug-covered platforms, with a view of the lake and the swans floating across its surface. They were mad Frank Zappa fans; that's all they played, though I don't think they understood a single lyric. "My dick is a Harley," growled Frank in the background, "you kick it to start."

Sandye seemed to be pairing off with the short, funny one, but I wasn't paying much attention. I was fascinated by his friend, a dark beauty from the Romansh part of

Switzerland, a bastion of Gypsies with its own, Romansh language. Suddenly I wanted him very badly, and I could tell he wanted me, too.

It was almost like losing my virginity again, sleeping with the perfectly formed Gypsy in his maroon-curtained bed. It was as if I had been holding my breath too long, dizzy and high on air. There was all this Christian imagery floating around in my head, too, from visiting churches and from the whole European experience. I felt like a nun who'd run away from the convent, anguished and pulsating. When he touched me, my brain was flooded with images of water and wet white feathers.

After that, Sandye and I were on a tear together, which was much more fun. Back in England, we picked up some on-the-dole Liverpudlians in a bar and slept in their tent in a field outside Cambridge. Mine was very thin and very pale, with hollow cheeks. They tried to steal our camera, but sheepishly gave it back when we couldn't find it to take group pictures before we left. When I got home there was a letter waiting from my thin friend; he had some fantasy about coming to the States. We would live in a little trailer, he thought.

But by this time I was too busy going to college, which had turned out to be more interesting than I first thought.

• • •

Sandye ended up at a little art school in Lake Placid that fall, and when she had to make a self-portrait for photography class, she had me come up to pose with her for a booklet of pictures of the two of us with my Olds Cutlass. This featured shots of us half naked, strapped to the roof rack with bungee cords; shots of us in the trunk; and in the last photo, the two of us standing in the road, fierce and shirtless, arms around each other, giving the poor beleaguered car the finger. The intended theme was our liberation from the great oppressor General Motors, but the end result more clearly featured boobs and bondage. This was about the time we French-kissed on the side of the Garden State Parkway, which was my idea. I was considering converting to lesbianism since girls seemed to like me better than boys did.

We got through this period pretty painlessly, but we did have other problems, usually caused by her moodiness, my neediness, or various contretemps involving other friends and relatives. Sandye has always been very honest in expressing her opinion and I have always been oversensitive. For a long time I worried that she didn't like my writing, or my outfit, or the color I'd painted my room, or whatever. Well, she didn't, at least not always, but why should she have to? At some point in life, I finally got enough confidence to stop minding.

For a few years we lived in an extremely crowded apartment in New York with my sister and her boyfriend and a changing cast of houseguests and overnight visitors, and those of us who are still alive would probably agree that this wasn't the greatest idea. Allegiances were confusing, phone bills were hard to divide, and everyone was taking too many drugs and sleeping with the wrong people and getting on one another's nerves. Finally I got so messed up that Sandye dragged me down to Mardi Gras to recover— our idea of a rest cure at the time. And this is when I met my beloved ice-skating bartender, my first husband; and though Sandye didn't come with us on our honeymoon, she did come on every trip we took after that. Once, in Florence, both she and Tony got in a bad mood simultaneously. I thought my brain would explode. But still I couldn't go much of anywhere without both of them.

The older we have gotten, the more we have prized our friendship and the less we would ever let anything bad happen to it. We have fixed most of the old things, too. Even if that newsletter was about me, I don't mind. And Sandye thinks I'm a really great writer now, don't you, San? While I think we have both worried about each other a lot, these days we have less to worry about, especially since we both stopped drinking a few years ago. Best of all, though it looked for a while like Sandye might never get to have a baby, now she has. In fact, we had daughters this year just a couple of months apart. Sandye Fern has Ava Peach.

One time we were discussing the fact that we would do anything for each other. I was trying to think of more and more preposterous challenges, like if my car broke down in Buffalo and she was in Kansas, would she come get me? She assured me that she would. After a while I really believed it. And now whenever everything goes wrong, I consider the fact that Sandye will come get me in the middle of the winter night in Buffalo, no matter how far away she is. And she has shown up, like magic, almost every time.

If you can find and keep a friend like this, it will be as precious as any other love you have, as precious as family, and certainly as precious as a Lamborghini, a house in the south of France, or the Nobel Prize. The companionship and continuity and unconditional love of a lifelong best friend is like a hearth fire always burning in one corner of your life, there to sit beside for a night of jokes and stories, or just when you've been out in the cold too long and you need a place to warm your hands.

Let's say your life is a museum. I recommend you spend at least as much time curating and conserving the Relationships Wing as the Cool Stuff Collection or the Trophy Room, and probably more, but this is not to put down stuff or trophies. I'm not going to go all ascetic on you, as I would have in my Hindu phase, and proclaim that our toys and games are samsara—illusions and dreams that will vanish when we truly awaken. Of course they will, but since I've decided not to wake up anytime soon if I can help it, I have come to a much closer relationship with my samsara.

Ah, the cool stuff. The toys. Your clothes, your house, your car, your plants, your books and music, your computer. Your comfy chair and reading lamp and magazine; the fresh-washed pillowcase and gently blowing curtain by your bed. Material possessions can certainly be the source of enormous pleasure. Enjoying them doesn't have to be all about conspicuous consumption, brand names, logos, insatiable desire. In fact, the pleasure in these objects is mostly the pleasure in the activities that surround them: choosing, using, maintaining them, and finally even letting them go. To do these things is to enact a personal aesthetic. It is the way we make beauty and comfort and pleasure part of our everyday lives.

Of course, some enjoy these activities more than others. While my son Hayes could spend a whole weekend studying sneaker catalogs and my friend Liz Lambert looked at three shades of tomato red for several hours to choose the color for a door, I tend to be a snap-decision, kamikaze shopper. For me, the fewer choices the better—I just want to get out of the store as fast as possible. I once bought a new refrigerator over the telephone, sight unseen, and selected my car by virtue of the fact that its dealership was the only one open on the day I went out to look. You sell cars? Great. Could I have one? And while the shopping people often take loving care of their possessions, I am a little handicapped in this department as well.

The care that things demand can be a kind of spiritual practice. My buddy and one of my favorite writers, Naomi Nye, wrote an essay about this called "Maintenance," and some of the images she offered have stayed with me always: plunging her hands into hot, hot water to wash dishes, for example. Her claim to find deep satisfaction in this has made me somewhat more inclined to enjoy it myself, though I am still unconvinced by her enthusiastic report of dusting the top lip of a door molding or the front edge of a bookshelf.

Basically, though, I'm for it. Go ahead and love your stuff. But face it, your stuff will not love you back. Your stuff will not pick you up in Buffalo. Your stuff will not clean your house and cook you dinner when you are incapacitated by loss or when you've just had a baby. Your stuff will not call you to see what you are doing for your birthday. And even your love of your stereo is more truly your love for another human voice.

• • •

What about that Trophy Room? The achieving, doing, accomplishing, and succeeding? Your awards and prizes, your curriculum vitae, your good jobs well done? I'll admit, I have been a little more stuck in this part of the museum than in the Cool Stuff Collection. Because while I tend to float just a few inches above the crass material plane (or I would if I didn't have to spend so much time crawling around the floor looking for lost contact lenses and such), I have been very tangled up with ambition and pride of talent. I have been so identified with my abilities and endeavors that at times I mistook them for my heart and soul.

For example, I used to think that if I didn't write, my life would be totally meaningless and no one would like me. The fact that I was a writer was the core of my identity, I thought, my saving grace. But I thought this thought so hard and so long and made such a big deal out of it that early in my twenties I worried myself to death, creatively speaking. I had no ideas, no material, or at least none strong enough to withstand the weight of this federal case I was making. And boy, did I complain.

It was as if I thought you could still be a writer if you replaced sitting on your butt typing with talking a lot about writing. I will have more to say about this later on, but for now, let me mention only that the situation got so nauseating that I finally decided I should quit writing, officially and publicly. Since I wasn't writing anyway this wasn't going to be that much of a change. Really all I was dropping was the complaining.

I had recently read a book called *Stones for Ibarra,* by Harriet Doerr, the author's first novel, written in her seventies. In her seventies? Well then, I had lots of time. I could just forget the whole thing until my seventies, then write prizewinning novels. And since the interviews I had read made it pretty clear that her sudden success did not rest on decades of bitching, perhaps I would have to shut up in the interim and find something else to do. There had to be another way to have a meaningful life.

Though I knew I couldn't count on the Doerr effect and still thought I might be quitting writing "forever," I don't think many of my friends or family members believed me. In fact the hiatus lasted about four years. But once it ended and I was working again, I was no longer so misguided. I knew that the most important thing in my life was taking care of myself and the people I loved. I knew, further, that those people didn't love me because I was a writer. And as for making things, I found cooking could be as much fun as writing, and I loved to draw, and I had a very demanding job at Morgan Jones's software company, which involved lots of hard work and creativity and which I actually liked quite a lot. There were dozens of things in my life that needed attention and care, and soon there were babies, the ultimate in this category, and maybe that's why I could start writing again: because once you're a mother, you can never think something else is the most important thing.

Back in the eighties, and thanks to that tomato red connoisseur Liz Lambert, I became friends with the women in the band Two Nice Girls. In fact this group had three and then four women in it, and one of them was Kathryn Korniloff. Korn, as her friends have always called her—the postmetal band of that name was a much later phenomenon—is one of those low-key, subtle people who have always fascinated me. There is an indirection, an elusiveness to her way of handling her emotions and her gifts and her intellect that is so different from my noisy barreling along. I have always felt I could learn something from her, or at least wished she would rub off on me.

A founding member of Two Nice Girls, Korn played guitar and sang and wrote songs with the band the six and a half years they were together, and also did the mailing list and the bookkeeping and the bookings and dozens of other non-rock-star tasks of that ilk. During this time, Two Nice Girls went from being beloved in the Austin music scene to being internationally known as lesbian folk rockers. They toured extensively, played huge festivals and tiny clubs, and put out three CDs. Though never a big success financially, they always put on a great show; their loose, silly, endless intersong patter was an entertainment phenomenon in itself.

Though their breakup was a rather acrimonious and lengthy process, as band breakups often are, the other day Korn commented that the period she was in Two Nice Girls was the happiest of her life so far.

I assumed it was because she was playing and writing music for an audience, achieving the goals so many musicians have but never reach. She agreed that she has never been more creatively fulfilled than she was then. But, she went on, the real joy of being in the band came from the relationships: the intense closeness she had with the women she played with and the bond they shared with their audience.

This was before the coming out of Melissa Etheridge, k.d. lang, or Ellen DeGeneres, Korn explained, and the band members had the very real sense that they were actively creating a community around their music. At that time, openly lesbian and gay musicians tended to remain within the rich but nevertheless closed circuit of queer festivals and cultural events. Two Nice Girls was part of that network, but they also went out into the straight world, playing regular rock clubs. There, die-hard lesbian fans mixed and mingled with straight audiences and all were disarmed by the band's humor, their guitar chops, and their political incorrectness.

The rock critic Michael Corcoran once wrote about how powerful it was to be in their audience alongside straight college boys and lesbians, singing the band's anthem, "I Spent My Last Ten Dollars on Birth Control and Beer." (The next line: "My life was so much simpler when I was sober and queer.") As the audience connected with Two Nice Girls, they connected with one another in a new way, in a way that included gays and straights yet kept lesbianism as the focus of the celebration. To be at the center of that experience, articulating it and personifying it, was both a thrill and a deep satisfaction.

As far as success and achievement were concerned, the band was never concerned about that as an end in itself. Because they had no illusions of fame and fortune, they were free to blow it out and have a great time being who they were. And that's the very thing that brought them the notoriety they did achieve.

For Korn, being a rock star wasn't about seeing her name in the paper or getting rich, or even about self-expression and creative achievement, but about people.

And the downfall of the band was about people, too. When the relationships stopped working, when the overfed egos started bumping into one another, when the carelessness and cockiness set in, everything else stopped working, too. And the loss of it left a hole in everyone's life.

That's the way it always is. Relationships are at the heart of every creative and business endeavor, and if you forget that you'll see those endeavors dry up. When it stops being about the people and turns into being about the products or the profit, it's no fun anymore. That's certainly what happened at our software company after Morgan sold it to some buttoned-down types from Silicon Valley. It's just a job. It's just a business. It's just a band. And soon it isn't even that.

Your possessions won't love you back and your achievements turn to dust without the red blood of human relationships coursing through them, which is why I urge you to take care of the people in your life. When you have to make a choice, put them first. This is the simplest way to be both a more ethical person and a happier person, both better and better loved. It even works for decisions of less moral weight, like choosing a college. If you base your decision on the sense you get of the people who go there, what they care about and what they do for fun, rather than the institution's status or the number of books in the library, you're more likely to end up in a place that's right for you.

Unless you are aiming for sainthood, you don't have to love everybody, or even like them. I don't. But when I do care about someone, I do the best I can to give them attention and love, and I have made a lifelong effort to keep friendships alive over long distances and separations. Sometimes people say I am lucky to have such good friends, but it is more than luck: it is a matter of lavishing time and energy on them, the way others do on their closets or their cars and their projects. And it's also because, at least at this point in my life, I am most interested in people who know how to love me back, who are interested in going to the places I want to go. Those are the ones who stick around.

Even our family members or the other people we live with don't tend to get the face time they need unless we consciously commit to giving it to them. I say "face time" because I have a three-month-old baby now and it's very clear that this is what she would like us to take the time to do: look into her face and let her look into ours. We smile, we gurgle, we raise our eyebrows, but mostly we just see and are seen. This simple, pure interaction is the most stripped-down version of communication, of play, of what two people can do for each other. I think we all want a lot more of that than we get, or are brave enough to even ask for.

In the end, it's sort of ridiculous to even compare achievements or possessions to the relationships we have with other people, since relationships are so much richer and more complicated. It's almost as if they have a dimension the other two lack. Because every time we experience caring for a person, it teaches us something about what is actually going on here. A very close relationship takes us to the edge of what we can know about someone else, and how deeply we can be known by them. Our love for the ineffable thing that another person is is a way of traveling toward that ineffable thing—which you might call a soul, or you might call God, or you might leave unnamed. This is information about the mysteries of life, and there is no way a stereo or a line on your résumé can possibly compete.

But there can be a dark side to what relationships teach us about being human. With so much on the table, much is at risk; and that is why this is the place we get hit the hardest. It hurts when your house burns down, it hurts when you don't get a job you wanted really badly, but someone you love can hurt you ten thousand times more than that. And even if they never hurt you in any way they can control, they could die or get hurt themselves and that would break your heart.

This is why, while you're out there loving people, you better be sweet to yourself, too. Because you, too, are more important than achievements or possessions, and you are what you'll be left with when all else fails. If you spend all your time taking care of other people without taking care of you—working and playing in ways you enjoy, buying yourself presents—you'll end up feeling resentful and narrow and used up.

Too much unselfishness tends to backfire. If you don't believe me, ask your mom.

Be gentle with your parents

4

When I launched into this one at the high school, I really felt I was wasting my breath. I knew how rebellious and difficult my sister and I had been as young people, and I couldn't imagine anything anyone could have said to us to change that. It wasn't just that we gave my parents trouble; we gave them trouble on purpose.

The job of growing up entails breaking away from Mom and Dad, and it isn't pretty. Starting in adolescence, all but a few of us keep secrets from our parents, disobey them, hurt them, and disown them in our heads. Eventually we may decide that one or both of them are screwed up and the whole family is dysfunctional. We may be right.

This process of separation—which can feel painful and destructive on both sides—starts in adolescence. But there's a reconstructive process, too, that goes on in parallel, though it may take a bit longer to get under way. It involves forgiving our parents, lightening up on them, and even possibly falling in love with them all over again, but as independent adults this time instead of helpless babies.

Like the crueler part of growing up, reconciliation with your parents can begin without your being quite aware of it. You leave home, move into your own place, think you're finally on your own—then begin to notice the ways you've taken them with you. Whoa, you think, they're still here, as their little voices speak to you from inside your head. At some point, key realizations about mortality and money also intervene, and if you have kids yourself, you really get a new perspective on the parental experience. It was hard! They tried! You were a brat!

Finally you get it: They're parents. They can't help being the way they are. It's annoying, but it's also irreplaceable.

In the summer of 1976, when I was a lass of eighteen, I paid a visit with my sister, Nancy, and best friend, Sandye, to Diamond Glen's Tattoo Parlor in Austin, Texas. Diamond Glen was understandably surprised to see us: back then, tattooing was still mostly for drunken sailors, gang members, and jailbirds, not teenaged Jewish girls from New Jersey.

I went first and got a little Sanskrit om character inside my right ankle. Diamond Glen balanced my foot on his knee and bent over it intently, a lock of his dark, slicked-back hair coming loose and dangling over his face. The tattooing tool buzzed in its merry, threatening fashion and I soon realized I found the experience exciting, even vaguely sexy. It didn't hurt at all! I reported—or only a little, in a good way.

Nancy went next. She got a rose on her upper arm. In her opinion, it hurt quite a lot and not necessarily in as good a way as previously asserted. Sandye's tattoo was a fern in her cleavage. She almost passed out. Apparently the hurt factor depends on where you get it and how much your brain can twist what pain you feel into something thrilling or erotic.

So, all done. Om, rose, fern. The next item on the agenda was a call to my mother. I dialed collect from Diamond Glen's phone. Guess what, Mommy! I blurted.

You're kidding, she said when I told her, then said she felt sick to her stomach.

Oh, what could be better? We had made our mother sick to her stomach.

My aunt Ellen recently described my mother as having more than nine lives. Among the near-fatal threats to her existence Ellen listed, along with heart attacks and cancer, were "you girls." I think it was a fair characterization. We were wild teenagers, and the seventies were a heyday for teenage wildness. Many of the adults were too busy with pot parties and wife swapping and other such seventies-type pursuits to pay attention to what we were up to, anyway.

I doubt it was my sister's idea to call my mother about our tattoos. She would surely have preferred to keep the details of our drug abuse, sex lives, and other misadventures from our parents, but I was a compulsive teller. The bad girl in me wanted to break the rules, and the good girl wanted to tell on her. It was as if my mother were my confessor or, even more, my disembodied superego. I had no regard for how this might have affected her. In fact, if she reacted with concern or hurt or disapproval, I jumped down her throat.

I was never gentle with my mother or my father, and my father did not live long enough to see the change in me (in fact, he died when I was at my most egregious, in frequent need of rescuing and affirmation). But I have changed, at last, by degrees, and sometimes in big jumps. Here's one way I can tell this has happened: I recently got my husband's initials tattooed on my right shoulder blade and *I have not told my mother about it.* This is my third tattoo; a few years ago, I got a blue dolphin leaping out of some green waves on my upper butt, or lower hip, depending on which way you're coming from. This I showed her right away. Look, Mom, I'm kooky as ever.

So why wouldn't I tell my mother about the initials? Look, Mom, I'm an impulsive romantic who has found her soul mate! Unfortunately, I think she will see it otherwise. She will think it is unbelievably stupid and ridiculous and may even get sick to her stomach. I just don't want that anymore. I know that it makes her happy to think I'm all grown up and sensible now, and I hate to ruin it by proving I'm the same moron I ever was. And maybe I've also started to realize how her opinion tends to inexorably affect me, sometimes over time even replacing my own, and I just don't want to sully my beautiful pure tattoo with those thoughts. If I want to hear what she thinks I can consult the Inner Mommy who resides permanently in my head, providing endless mommyesque commentary on my own and other people's behavior. It's like those people who wear bracelets that say, *What Would Jesus Do?*—only mine is, *What Would Mommy Say?* Since I know damn well, why give the poor woman a stomachache?

Internalizing your parents so that your nastiest dialogues go on completely in your head is one way of starting to be more gentle with them in real life. Moving out of their house is a big help, too. If they don't have to see that filthy / threadbare / too tight / too big / ridiculously expensive pair of jeans you're wearing, or become acutely

99

aware of the amount of time you spend on the phone / on the Internet / in the bathroom, they won't be forced to comment on these things, and there goes a good third of the static, if not more.

While both merging with your parents psychologically and separating from them physically are useful steps toward treating them more gently, these things may be a bit ahead of you in the future. In the meantime, there are a few simple concepts you can attempt to embrace to start the softening process.

1. Your parents will not live forever, and neither will you.

2. They really cannot help all their attempts to fix, correct, and save you—that's what being a parent is.

3. They are more or less right about money.

As to your parents not living forever, I have quite a bit to say.

After my father died, when I was twenty-seven, I was a lot more appreciative of my mother. For about three months. Then things went back to normal—her asking if I got my doorbell fixed yet, me snapping her head off. I like my damn doorbell the way it is, don't you get it? Broken! That's how I want it! My stance on the issue went far deeper than laziness: I was simply not the kind of person who got my doorbell fixed. I was busy! And even if I hadn't been so

busy, I had bigger, less
like some people.

Don't even mention

Then one day last Mo

"I was just picking

knowing she was anxio

velopment in my work I

what more tolerable tho

was supposed to call h

I hadn't.

I know you've never

When Supposed to Syn

have, then, like me, you

hand. But putting all ex

ance the pleasantness

twists and turns in the

annoying aspect. Especi

take a d___b___ for a pl

In any case, making

the tale, and it wasn't

have to go soon and—"

"I'm almost done," I

"Yes, but I have some

I went rigid, the wo

words. "What?"

bourgeois things on my mind. Not

he doorbell again, okay?

, I got a call from her.

p the phone to call you," I said,

s to hear the latest on a little de-

fe, an interest that I found some-

n the one in my d__b___. Anyway, I

r the minute I knew anything, but

experienced Failure to Call Mother

rome, and if by some chance you

had a plethora of excuses right at

uses aside, one always has to bal-

of one's mother's interest in the

ot line of one's life with its faintly

lly if she has the tendency to mis-

t element.

p for my tardiness, I launched into

ntil she broke in and said, "Well, I

aid.

bad news."

you do when people say those

When I was his age, a klutzy, messy little girl,
ally slightly terrifying. I would look at her and
from that? That trimness and slimness and
those teeth that practically glowed in the da

Back then, she reigned over her country c
champion of golf, not to mention her tenni
and if there had been a championship for
Times Sunday crossword puzzle, Mrs. Hyman
as her name occasionally appeared in the spo
that very paper, would have won it as well, her
across the page like she was writing a letter. S
energy, little patience, and was never less
frank in expressing her opinions, in whateve
might require and regardless of audience. Mo
athlete, sports fan, stock market expert, r
books, she was the mom who came in from
politics were Republican all the way, with no
poor schleppers in this country or any other. Is
ment in business to fix all the injustices o
Please.

When we were little, my sister and I used t
tend game where we put on bright coral lipsti
of penny loafers and stamped around the ho
ing, "Jesus Christ! Jesus Christ!" Guess who? T
serious cooking and cleaning in our home was

he was actu-   g once, behind the
think, I came   elevision, the Mets
smoothness,   l try?" I asked.
?   n to iron, that's my
ub as ladies'   er let anyone know
and bridge,   ing kept the iron in
he *New York*   a play. She set the
Jinik (Jane),   arette. "Watch this
ts section of
hand moving   pretended to watch.
e had lots of   ghout my childhood
than utterly   *f matches—we were*
words they   *then I got out of the*
tini drinker,   *the four wood to the*
ader of guy   phrases run through
e cold. Her   of the Latin mass for
ympathy for   s, took lessons, and
the govern-   use, like sleep-away
the world?   had enjoyed and as-
              I was terrible at all of
play a pre-   e do it.
k and a pair   m my mother in early
se exclaim-   drive up Ocean Av-
ough all the   le, coming home from
done by the   cor, or maybe my psy-

chiatrist, screaming, "I hate you, Mommy," and I remember her pulling into the driveway and saying, "I hate you, too." (If you ask her she will say this didn't happen, but it did, and when I think of how difficult I was back then, I hardly even blame her.)

It was very important to me that I be nothing like my mother. Like my dashing hilarious libertine father, fine, but not like her. Even in my thirties, I made a little list of her character traits on a yellow Post-it note at work, just to prove to myself that I was the opposite in every way. She was cautious, negative, pessimistic, suspicious; I was none of these things. She made pot roast with onion soup mix and ketchup but I was a great cook. Even my coleslaw was imaginative. Once when she was down to visit me in Texas, when my children were very small, she watched me chop dill and watercress and do something arcane with umeboshi plums and asked if I really had to put so many ingredients in the coleslaw.

It was almost that day in the Le Mans all over again.

Over time, we have both changed. I've got the Inner Mommy now, and often I sound like her ("You have a new boyfriend? What does he do?"), think like her ("A lawyer? That's good!"), and even dress like her. Well, she keeps giving me all these blazers and pants and old evening dresses she can't use anymore, and I must say I wear them. I put on an emerald green floor-length Qiana tank dress— Qiana was one of those seventies synthetics that didn't quite make it—to wear to a wedding, and I could just see her parading off to the golf club in it thirty years ago. So where were the sandals dyed to match? I called her and she sent them right out, UPS second day.

Oh, it gets worse. I watch both the NFL and the NBA on television. I have a cleaning lady, send my kids to camp, and inveigh frequently against credit card debt. You should see my hands—tan and veiny with her very same ridged fingernails.

I hardly ever make that coleslaw anymore.

She, on the other hand, has gone soft on us. Nana, as she is now known, often bakes cookies. She voted for Clinton. She's revealed some amazing stories of womanly passion. And nowadays she even pretends to need my help to do the crossword puzzle. Though she first reacted to the news of my pregnancy at forty-two with, "Jesus Christ, Marion," and shocked people with her negative response ("You must be so excited, both your daughters pregnant." "They're idiots."), she came around fast. When we found out it was a girl and decided to name it after her, as she named me after her mother, she started knitting a baby blanket.

I started calling her every day after that Wednesday in May when she told me the news about her lymphoma. I would tell her about my pregnancy, or about taking my car in for service, or about what I was going to wear to some wedding, suddenly not annoyed by her interest but acutely aware that absolutely no one else in the world would ever give a damn. She, in turn, would tell me about her wig, or the port in her chest, or her golf game. For as it turned out, she was playing right through chemo. Maybe only eleven holes, maybe in a cart, maybe bald and wearing a baseball cap, but playing nonetheless. And dining out, and going to Atlantic City, and watching *Jeopardy!* and *Wheel of Fortune* with even fiercer dedication and pleasure than usual.

In fact, my mother was getting unusual pleasure from many things. In one phone call, she launched into a detailed description of a lobster stuffed with crabmeat and vermouth she had eaten at a dinner party.

"It was the best lobster I ever had in my life," she told me.

Well, I could believe that. But when she told me she had gotten up the next morning and had "the best bagel with egg and cheese I ever had in my life, at"—you're not going to believe this—"McDonald's," I knew my New York Jew of a mother was having a profound response to her situation.

I had heard, of course, that some people respond to a diagnosis of terminal illness with renewed zest for life, patience, love, and spirit. But I had never seen it happen. For example, I had watched my first husband die slowly of AIDS, and I have to say terminal illness really didn't do much for his personality, bless his heart. But here was my mother, eating the best bagel of her life at McDonald's. And she was still talking about it. "Remember how Daddy and I used to love those Egg McMuffins? This was so much better than that."

"I miss Daddy," I said suddenly, because I did.

"Me, too," she said emphatically. I was taken aback. It's not that I didn't think she missed him, but I never heard her say it in the sixteen years since his death.

From then on, I looked forward to our phone calls with secret hilarity, to see what she would come up with next. One day she told me about Diane and Leon Katz's fiftieth anniversary party, held at the golf club. She and a few other friends had worked hard to make it festive, planning a special menu, bringing in flowers and a cake and Diane's favorite candy, everything just right. "They lost the candy," she said. "And we had ordered the lobster steamed, but they stuffed it with some kind of thermidor. When they took Ceddie's order, he said, 'I'll have the same,' meaning the lobster, and then they misunderstood and brought him the salmon. I mean, everything went wrong that possibly could have gone wrong."

"Oh my God," I said. I knew she must have been furious. Being furious at the management of the golf club dining room had been a major pastime of my parents since my earliest youth. I steeled myself for the firestorm.

"It was the funniest thing I ever saw," she said.

"It was?"

"Oh, you just had to laugh," she said.

"You did?"

I really could not believe my ears. My mother had become the freaking Buddha.

My mother continued doing incredibly well throughout her chemo. She wasn't nauseated, she wasn't tired; in fact, she was fine. When my little Jane was born, in late June, she couldn't wait for the day my aunt was supposed to drive her over to Pennsylvania, and she jumped in the car and came the three hours herself. After nine weeks, chemo was over and she was to start radiation. She was to go every day for a month. It wasn't easy; she really was having trouble fitting radiation into her schedule. Morning appointments blew her golf dates; afternoon cut into bridge. We had come a long way from that first phone call, where she wasn't playing golf all summer (or as I'm sure we both thought, ever).

Before she started radiation, she had a scan to check the progress of her treatment. She was injected with a dye that turned the lymphoma cells bright orange, and when they went to look at them the next day, there weren't any.

"Can you believe it?" she said.

"No," I said, stunned, speechless, and really, really happy. "But yes."

I am afraid to think of it as more than a temporary reprieve. But so far, it has been an amazing one. The very next day, my mother played in the finals of the Better Ball of Partners at her beloved golf club. It was an important tournament and there had been a large gallery, a brigade of senior citizens in golf carts following the match.

"I was the Jane Winik of twenty years ago," she said, and gave me the hole-by-hole, just as that Jane Winik would have.

She had parred three, four, ten, thirteen, fifteen, sixteen, and seventeen. She had a forty-one on the back nine. Her putting had been sensational; her partner, who had carried them through the first rounds of the tournament, was thrilled. And then there was eighteen, a par five. "It all came back to me," she said. "All the times I've stood on that tee, all those championships, all those memories."

She hit a good first shot, a good second shot. At that point, all four players had the same lie and there was a big nasty trap between them and the hole. One after the other, the players went into it. "I hit a seven iron to the green and two-putted to win," she said.

I almost knew what she was talking about.

"People were crying," she said.

I didn't blame them. I was crying myself. "Are you celebrating?"

"Well, right now I'm just killing time until I go over for radiation," she said. "I would be watching *Jeopardy!* but your sister's son messed up the programming on my VCR."

Oh no.

"Ah," she said. "So what? No big deal."

Perhaps this would be a good time to tell her about the tattoo, after all.

Speaking of tattoos, my husband, Crispin, has six, at least last time I looked. Two of them, the owl and the rose, are in memory of his two brothers that died. And I think he would trace some of his pronounced and endearing gentleness with his parents to the time of their deaths.

When Crispin was twelve and his younger brother, Adam, was ten, their mother remarried and they acquired two rather wild teenage stepbrothers: Jim and Bob. By the time Crispin was thirty-two, he had helped bury two of those boys on their parents' farm in Virginia. First Bob, who was murdered by a friend of his during a drug-fueled argument (after shooting Bob, the young man immediately drove Bob's truck into a tree and died too). Crispin was nearby when it happened. He found Bob's bloody body lying in the road.

A few years later, Adam died of a heroin overdose in his grandmother's apartment—whether it was intentional or accidental or some combination of the two, his family wonders to this day. I never met him so I can only tell you these few things: He was a deejay and a modern music freak, a connoisseur of champagne, Thai food, and hand-thrown ceramic objects, a really good chess player. He was only thirty and he was Crispin's little brother.

While it is common to dread the loss of our parents, since it seems bound to occur at some point, we don't usually give that much thought to what it would be like for our parents to lose us—this is not supposed to happen at all. When you see them go through that sort of agony, as Crispin did, it changes you. You realize that you have to take care of your parents and give them lots of love, even if you do have some complaints and criticisms and despite the fact they irritate the hell out of you sometimes. And part of what you have to do for them is take care of yourself, no matter how much it goes against your grain.

• • •

As to the essential need of parents to fix you:

There are people who wreck their cars and their parents don't lift a finger to help because they feel their kid needs to deal with the consequences of their mistakes themselves.

There are other people who wreck their cars and their parents buy them a new car the next day because they understand that a person really needs to get around and they know their kid will be more careful next time.

Guess what. *Both* of these groups of people are pissed at their parents. Why? Because in both cases, the parents are just trying to help, and that fact alone is intolerable. The fact that we need help is the root of this intolerability. Ever since you knocked your rice cereal on the floor because you didn't want your mother leering at you and playing that stupid choo-choo game with the spoon when you were certainly capable of eating breakfast yourself, you have been angry about your dependency on these big, well-meaning galoots who call themselves your parents. When you are enraged by the fact of your need, whatever help is offered cannot be accepted with dignity. So, seventeen years later, even if they save you from immobility by giving you the new car, you will just mutter some cursory thanks and later tell people how they enabled your bad habits by buying you new cars every time you wrecked one.

Or let's say you are having a rather challenging young life. You are not getting the grades you should, or you are in trouble at school or work, or you have bad habits that will ruin your life if unchecked. Let's say you are kind of fat, and therefore don't get picked for any sports teams or don't get the boyfriends you would like. Let's say you got low test scores, or your best friend got a new best friend and you're out of the club.

A parent would have to be made of stone to sit by and watch these things happen to you without saying or doing anything. I know mine couldn't. They shipped me around to doctors and shrinks. They wondered if they should move me to private school. (These teenage crises are private schools' bread and butter, since changing your school is a relatively effortless, if costly, approach to fixing you. Of course, it rarely works, since the private school will probably just have more drugs, more snobs, and more social and academic pressure than wherever they yanked you from.) On the drug front, my parents tried taking our pot, telling us not to smoke pot, asking us to smoke pot only at home, et cetera. They didn't actually smoke pot with us, but I certainly know of parents who did this, too.

Here is the problem: parents can't accept that *nothing* they do is going to help, and we can't accept that they won't just shut up and go away. It is irremediable. And it is almost kind of funny.

Here's the bottom line: A parent (at least a healthy and sane parent) is programmed to care, feed, and nurture. They can't just turn it off when you reach the age where this solicitousness annoys you (eighteen months for some of us), or even the age where you rarely need it anymore. You can kind of expect them to wind down by the time you're in your forties or so—but on the other hand, there may be times when you really need them and you'll be glad they're there. For you, the great and powerful grown-up you, may need a short-term loan or a baby-sitter or—believe it or not—some comfort and advice, and perhaps you will be secure enough to ask for it with grace and receive it with gratitude.

But that security can be long in coming, and so is the parental restraint that allows its development. So in the meantime, be gentle.

As to the money:

There are many issues on which parents and kids disagree, and with most of these, the truth lies somewhere between. For example, most activities are not as dangerous as they think or as harmless as you think. One thing they are probably right about, though, is money. Because it's not that you don't need money and security and you don't have to conduct your life in a way that enables you to accrue those things. It's that when you're a kid and your parents do all those things for you, you can get the impression that they don't need to be done at all. That your parents are boring, hung-up people, and you are an exciting free person. The fact is that they would be a lot more exciting and free if they had someone to pay for everything for them, too. They would go to Paris for the weekend and order perfume off the Internet and just stay home in bed and watch movies whenever they felt like it.

This is part of the reason that you get along better with your parents once you move out of the house. Once you are on your own, the little price tag attached to every consumer good will become much more evident to you. You will gradually stop thinking such denigrating thoughts about savings accounts and insurance policies and the people who have them. You, too, will be rather anxious to prevent your more expensive possessions from getting lost or broken, and therefore having to be replaced. And you will also see that taking care of people financially really is a way of loving them, and not some kind of vulgar capitalist plot. You will realize that there are worse things to be than bourgeois or middle class. Like poor, for example.

This may not happen right away. Poor can be lots of fun while you are in your twenties, single, and childless. This is a good age for living with seven people in a two-bedroom apartment to save on rent, for eating the free food at art openings, for staying with people you happen to meet on the train when you're traveling. But gradually you will age, and you may appreciate a little more comfort and security. You will probably acquire a little raft of people and things you have to take care of and provide for, so when uncertainty looms, you will feel compelled to vanquish it. You will phone ahead. You will make reservations. Finally, you will succumb altogether, and the romance of poverty will be replaced in your mind by the romance of financial ease, as you find yourself having dreams concerning mutual funds. Sigh.

Until then, every time you borrow your parents' long distance credit card, their AAA membership, or their washing machine, say thank you as nicely as possible.

When I first became a parent, I was knocked over by the tidal wave of affection, concern, and attachment that I felt for my baby. It nearly moved me to tears to think my parents had felt this way about me. It's just so huge and all-encompassing—really it's almost superhuman, except that it's the essence of ordinary humanity—and when you think of your mother and father loving you with this fierce, inexorable passion, especially considering how everyone usually treats one another, it's sort of improbable and heartbreaking at the same time.

And the improbability continues, along with the poignancy. For example, the other day I pulled up to my sister's house for a visit, and my mother, who was already there, came out to greet us. She had a short, electric lavender afro and looked like a seventy-two-year-old white female Dennis Rodman. Apparently her hair had just started to grow back after chemo and something went wrong when she tried to dye it.

She walked around like that all weekend, Mom and her half-inch-long purple fro. She seemed rather proud of it.

We each get one mother and one father, and now I see: this one is all mine.

never stop doing
what you care about most

This is the career counseling section of this book, and we suggest total self-indulgence: you should do exactly what you love to do. Let me tell you why, and let me describe the interesting career paths of some of my unruly friends.

Then we'll talk about what you should do if you have no idea what you care about most, a much more common problem than you might think.

The surest way to become a dried-up, disillusioned, cranky asshole before you're even thirty is to let go of the things you love to do. You drag yourself off to work in the morning, you drag yourself home at night, and the rest of the time is taken up with chores and errands and maybe a football game on TV or a party you don't even want to go to, and pretty soon life is just a gray wash. This is why people have midlife crises, because they can take only about twenty years of this crap before they mutiny: buy a big black

Harley, go back to school or to Tibet, change jobs, change spouses, and basically just start swigging down experiences that stimulate them emotionally, mentally, and physically—which they should have never stopped having in the first place. These midlife crises are often described as a foolish attempt to feel young again, but there is nothing foolish about it. If by feeling young they mean feeling excited and glad to be alive, I think it's ridiculous to set an age limit.

If you can make money doing the thing you care about most, so much the better. But even if you remain an amateur, you must not stop doing it. Horseback riding, art, reading, travel, collecting something, playing a sport: nothing is too goofy or lofty or frivolous, and if someone tries to tell you it is self-indulgent to devote time to this pursuit of yours (this someone could well be a little voice in your own head), please know they are wrong. The things we love to do are as important to our lives as the things we do to pay the bills, and if we are so inclined, and lucky, and don't give up, we may be able to make them pay the bills after all.

Take me. I never thought I would make a living by writing. My family had no writers in it and I knew not one person who wrote even as an avocation, so naturally it did not seem like a real thing that ordinary people might do. And so while I was almost always doing some sort of writing, I also did other things to make money. I had my share of good luck with my work—two small-press books of poetry, several publications in journals, lots of readings—but none of them were a windfall of cash, or paid anything at all. Even when I started writing personal essays for the local alternative weekly, it was very much a don't-quit-your-day-job situation; I think my original rate at the *Austin Chronicle* was ten cents per column inch. I was always sending stuff off to national magazines and I got some nice rejection letters, but I bet I was closer to paying them than they were to paying me.

Finally, I did get some big breaks. Two magazines—*Parenting* and *American Way,* the in-flight magazine of American Airlines—each broke down and said I could do a piece for them. About the same time, Austin's local NPR reporter, John Burnett, suggested I read on *All Things Considered* some of the essays he'd read in the *Chronicle.* A literary agent heard one of them and suggested I put together a book. And then the NEA gave me a grant and a publisher wrote me a pretty big check, or so it seemed to me at the time.

It was suddenly right there in front of me, the life of a writer. But I was afraid to step off the ledge. I had held my computer software job for ten years by then, and though it was nowhere near the fun it had been in the early days—the company had been bought and sold and many of my friends had left—it was still a pretty cozy gig. As long as I kept it, I had a paycheck, I had benefits, I had security. If I left the job, I would have none of those. What if I never sold anything else? What if the book was a big bomb and I was a laughingstock?

Right around this time I had dinner with my friend Naomi Nye, the writer and duster of door moldings, and her husband, Michael. Naomi and I were doing an article together for *Parenting* about traveling with children to Austin and San Antonio. These were our hometowns, so we didn't actually need to go anywhere to write the piece. That was just wrong, I thought; I was sure being a travel writer was supposed to include a certain amount of fun on the magazine's expense account. When Naomi told me there was a fancy French restaurant in San Antonio that offered child care while you dined, I insisted we try it.

I suppose the reason I remember all this in such detail is that the conversation we had that evening turned out to be one that changed my life. I was filling Naomi and Michael in on my situation and on the decision I faced about whether to leave my job and devote my time to writing. I had just about talked myself out of it, but perhaps I knew subconsciously that they were the people to bring me back around.

Michael had recently taken a year off from a very successful career as a lawyer to pursue photography. Not commercial photography, where people pay you to take pictures of their products or family members or weddings, but art photography, with no guarantees of remuneration whatsoever.

This was one of the more responsible and serious people I had ever met, hardly one to make such a decision lightly. Unlike other friends who'd taken every available detour on the way to maturity, Michael had stayed on the appointed path and schedule and had become just what his parents wanted him to be: a lawyer. He liked the practice of law, and he was good at it. But there was something else always in the back of his mind.

When Michael was in law school, he had visited an exhibit of work by two photographers, Paul Caponigro and Imogene Cunningham, and from that time, he had seen art in a new way. He put together a simple darkroom and started to balance the aggressive problem solving of law with the receptive observation of photography. In his spare time, he read biographies of photographers he admired. As he read, he began to realize that he was as attracted to the life of an artist as to taking pictures. He had to try it. And so he began to save everything he could to finance a year off.

Michael approached his project in a typically methodical, disciplined way. (He explained to me that having had serious dyslexia as a child has been surprisingly helpful to him in life. After a great deal of very hard work, he finally was able to read well at twelve—and that steady intensity of effort has never left him.) First he literally memorized the writings of Ansel Adams, generally thought of as the greatest technical photographer ever—outlined them, studied them, mixed the chemicals, tested the papers. Then he sat down and wrote letters to a half dozen of the photographers and art historians he admired most. He asked if he might come talk to them about their work, and his plan. Every one of them invited Michael to visit, and these meetings were pivotal in shaping his new life and his approach to his work.

Still, his decision to take a year off did not go unopposed. "This is the most ridiculous thing I've ever heard," some people told him. "You're a dreamer. And what about the income you'd be giving up?" He had no education in photography. His father, a judge on the Texas Court of Appeals, was so angry that he all but severed their relationship.

The other reaction he got was, "I wish I could do that . . . but I can't." The reasons given were legion, from "My spouse wouldn't like it" to "I'm too far in debt" to "They can't spare me at work."

Sitting there at dinner that night as he told me this story, I knew what every one of these excuses really meant: I'm scared.

But, Michael said, life is going by! Even the sensibility you have now—it'll be gone in five or ten years, replaced with a different way of perceiving and making things. The work you do in your twenties is not the work you do in your thirties. You use it or lose it.

After that first year, Michael knew that he was not going back to law full-time, though he continued to do consulting work part of the year. Now it is almost ten years after that conversation, and he has become known for his portraits of adults and children from troubled or impoverished areas around the globe: Siberia, Chiapas, Kurdistan, China, refugee camps in the Middle East. He has done series about mental illness, about teen parents, about his wife and baby sleeping, about old, old farmers on their land. And there is money in it now, at least enough for the simple life that he and Naomi lead, through workshops and grants and stipends, and people buying those startling, beautiful pictures to hang on their walls.

What Michael made me see that night is that what you have in life, essentially, is your time. If you sell your time to a company, you will get money, but you will not have that time anymore. It is simple: you sell it, or you keep it and use it in your own way.

Well, that was it for me. I quit my job in July of 1994 and I have not looked back. I got to be one of those people who are doing what they love for money. And it really isn't as rare as you would think. Crispin, sitting right across from me at the desk now, spends his time reading philosophy, biography, and history and teaches those subjects at an art school and writes books about them. He does opinion pieces about politics and about pop culture for several newspapers, as well as a monthly column about country music. He has always done these things, really—first as a grad student / rock critic in a ragbag bed-sit in London, now as a grown man with a fine home and five children to help take care of. I don't think he's ever had a real job, and this is probably best for all concerned. Not to say the guy is lazy—far from it. He is an obsessed and extremely ambitious workaholic who can write an op-ed column in the time it would take most people to turn on their computer and pour a cup of coffee. But I'm afraid he would be the world's balkiest mule if you tried to yoke him to some other cart. Crispin will never stop doing what he loves because for him there is no other thinkable way to live.

Part of being able to do what you love is seeing how it is done: having role models. Unlike me, who didn't meet a writer until I was in college, and Michael Nye, who mounted a letter-writing campaign in order to encounter real live photographers, Crispin virtually inherited the family business. His great-grandfathers and grandfathers on both sides were writers. His father was a reporter for the *Washington Star* and an editor at *National Geographic.* With all this going on in the family tree, becoming a writer must have seemed a natural thing to do, though he did face family opposition on going to graduate school and becoming a college professor. To his father this was no way to make a living. He saw writing as a trade, like TV repair; the last thing he wanted his son to be was a pointy-headed intellectual, or worse, a perennially impoverished doctoral candidate.

Well, a little family opposition was just the thing for this former high school revolutionary.

My old boss Morgan Jones was one of the crazy-ass entrepreneurs in faded jeans and beat-up running shoes who changed the world of computers in the eighties and nineties. Morgan barely finished high school and dropped out of college after one semester—then went on to become a whiz kid programmer, an ace computer salesman, and founder of an extremely successful software start-up. His career path seems to have been guided by a few key principles: If the rules are stupid, break them. If the place sucks, leave.

He dropped out of high school senior year because even with just one world history credit left, the school wouldn't let him go to a part-time work-study arrangement, claiming they would lose part of their federal funding. But Morgan already had a job at a print shop, where he'd worked since he was fifteen, and was already accepted at college, so he left. He worked days and finished world history at night school.

When he arrived at college, his freshman class in computer programming had four hundred people in it. The way it was going, he figured it would take them three years to write their first program. So he learned Fortran over a weekend, never attended this class again, and still made an A on the final. He left school altogether after that semester, figuring he could learn more and faster in the real business world.

He was still working with the printer, now keeping books and typing mailing lists. These were exactly the types of projects that computers were perfect for, so Morgan took a course at IBM to learn how to write the programs. Since Morgan's boss didn't have a computer, IBM arranged for him to use other people's systems at night. From the start, programming was like magic to him. He could type in a few keystrokes to try something out and a few seconds later see if it worked. When the machine did what he told it to, it hooked him like a drug. He would stay in those deserted offices until dawn.

After working briefly as a fireman, a waxer of airplanes at a private airport, and a shrimper on the Gulf coast, Morgan finally got a job where he got to play with his favorite toy, as a night computer operator. But the applications at the place where he worked were really badly written, so Morgan recoded them. When the programmers came in and saw what he'd done, they were furious. They tried to get him fired; instead he was offered a job running the place. A similar thing happened at his next employer, a class ring outfit. They had hired a Big Eight consultant to help them move all their systems to a mainframe computer. Morgan figured out how they could do it all on new mini computers from IBM, cutting the amount of space they needed for their headquarters and saving the company a million bucks. So long, Big Eight consultant.

Morgan was a troublemaker and he didn't care if he got canned, but somehow he never did. By his mid-twenties, he was in business for himself selling Hewlett-Packard computers. Quickly he and his partner became the largest HP resellers in the southern region and got known as software troubleshooters. The HP representative who took them around to problem sites, a country club Houstonite with major gold jewelry, had quite a job on her hands. She never knew on any particular plane flight if they'd pretend to be Irish priests, escaped mental patients, or (worse) themselves.

Morgan loved the high stakes and the risk of being a little-fish vendor in an ocean full of whales and sharks. Once, when HP offered a big rebate on past purchases if you reached a certain sales level by a certain date, he ordered four quarter-million-dollar computers—but he didn't actually have customers for them yet. Only by conducting a feverish, 24/7, no-holds-barred sales effort did he find them homes before payment was due to HP.

By 1980, he realized that the applications and utilities he had created for his customers could be packaged and sold separately. This is when he founded Tymlabs, the software company at which I toiled so happily for so many years. By the mid-nineties, his knack for motivating other people, his insights about the future of computers, and his truly maniacal drive and perfectionism made him a millionaire. That's when he claimed to be "retiring"—and I already told you how that turned out in Chapter 2, "Mistakes Need Not Be Fatal."

What's missing from this story? The women. Morgan truly loves the company of women and happily declares that he never did a single thing in his life that wasn't directly or indirectly aimed at making him more attractive to the opposite sex. Knowing the man, and his long string of lovely and intelligent companions, I don't doubt it. People have run for president for similar reasons.

Some sell computers; others start with sunglasses. That's what Sandye ended up doing after art school. One day her senior year she met a guy who'd just bought an old sunglasses factory and was converting it to make safety goggles. He mentioned that he'd found quite a bit of the old inventory in storage. Sandye asked if she could go look—and there they were, a warehouse full of fifties and sixties sunglasses in mint condition. She bought a few hundred pairs of them at ten cents apiece, thinking she'd sell them somewhere in her travels. But the first place she stopped, Canal Jeans in New York, bought every single pair. She went right back up to Johnstown and bought some more. Over the next three years, she sold about ten thousand pairs of those glasses—all there were.

It sort of amazed me, the way Sandye would just drive around a town until she detected a cool store, walk in with her samples, and start selling. She told me she got the idea from her cousins Kenny and Phyllis, with whom we had stayed in Cannes during our trip to Europe. These two were flogging watches with your initials in tiny gold letters on the face: the hottest thing on the Riviera that summer. If they could do it, Sandye thought, surely she could. Though not the typical entrepreneur in that she always seemed determined to make the least possible profit—the girl is a commie, what can I say?—she definitely had the run-your-own-business gene. Her grandma had a women's clothing store in Brooklyn, her dad owned a car place, her mom knitted baby booties on consignment, and I'm sure their nomadic ancestors sold tents in the desert.

She was out visiting stores in Greenwich Village with the last of the sunglasses. A lady with a shop on West Fourth Street wanted them all, but she didn't have cash. She asked if Sandye would take a gross of panty hose in trade.

A gross of panty hose. *White* panty hose. Others would have flinched. Sandye took the panty hose home and started playing with some handmade stencils and fabric ink. Soon she had a line of handprinted legwear for men, women, and children. They had palm trees or blenders or dinosaurs or hammers and saws or abstract images, each of which Sandye printed by hand and then ironed to set. In my recollection, she spent several years in our crowded little hot-box apartment standing at the ironing board, making her panty hose and watching old movies on our tiny black-and-white TV. The same stores that had snapped up the sunglasses went crazy for the socks and stockings, and soon Sandye was shipping orders all over the country, doing every bit of work herself and charging bottom dollar.

After five years she was really, really sick of panty hose. The work had gotten tedious, and the fashion world, which she had begun to get to know, was on the one hand shallow and greedy and on the other being devastated by AIDS. She decided to pack it in and take a job cooking at an Italian restaurant near our apartment. It was quite a good restaurant and Sandye became an accomplished chef in the years she worked there.

Meanwhile, Sandye had not given up ceramics, her love since art school. In the basement of her parents' house in New Jersey, she set up a studio and a kiln, and made hand-built pitchers, candlesticks, flowerpots, and other functional pieces that she painted with beautiful designs and patterns. Some of these she took around to the faithful stores that had been selling her wares all along—and they loved them. Especially the flowerpots.

This was almost ten years ago, and now Sandye is getting a little sick of flowerpots. While all this entrepreneurship has been fun, she feels she's never really gotten to do her art the way she wanted to. She even recently wondered aloud if she should have let her parents support her after she got out of school, as some of her classmates did, while she tried to establish a real career as an artist.

But it's not too late. These days she's running a bed-and-breakfast in Brooklyn in a funky old building she and her man, Rik, have fixed up. If the inn business makes enough money (questionable, since, as you can imagine, she's got the cheapest lodging rates in New York), she wants to go back to hand-building ceramics again. Finally, she says, she'll get to be an artist.

I think she always has been. Not just as the creative force behind the flowerpot and panty hose patterns, but as the designer of the way she's lived her life.

So many people care deeply about politics and social issues when they are young—and so few retain those passions as they move into adulthood. What happens to most of us is that we get distracted by making money and having children, and soon our ideals are just something to be nostalgic about, like a band we used to love or a summer job we once had. Some lose interest in public matters altogether; others find their views transformed completely once they have a family and a business to take care of. The plight of the world strikes us every day when we read the paper and listen to the news, but unless it affects us directly, we usually limit our response to sending out a check.

I do know a few people who have been able to translate their youthful caring and commitment into some life activity, thus retaining a core of meaning in their lives where many feel hollow. Jennifer, another friend from college, has never stopped working for peace and justice and human decency, from a soup kitchen in Los Angeles back when we were still practically teenagers to a Central American refugee center in Austin today. Living her whole life with heart wide open, she married a guy who is the same way; he's now a lawyer defending the rights of those on death row.

Our friend Jeff Joslin—you know, the one with the motorcycle and the biodegradable sleeping bag—has had about the most street-corner-to-corner-office résumé I know of. Politics has always been an obsession with him; he remembers visiting our college as a high school senior during a student takeover of the administration building and thinking, This is the place for me!

But by the time Jeff got there in the fall, the student leaders had gone off to law school and all was quiet on the quad, except for the occasional frat party. Like me, he spent as much time as possible that year off campus, but while I was chanting mantras in New York City, he was community organizing and getting arrested in various union picket lines at local hotels and supermarkets.

At the end of the year, he dropped out to join the fight to shut down the construction of the Seabrook nuclear power plant in New Hampshire. In the most colorful of almost weekly arrests at the plant site, 1,414 protesters were dragged into buses and held in national guard armories while the governor tried to figure out what to do. The state could no longer afford to feed them. During this internment, Jeff met a bunch of students and their teachers from the Goddard College Institute for Social Ecology, in Vermont—the only college in America where alternative energy systems, environmental design, and anarchist theory were being taught as a single curriculum. Now *this* is the place for me, he thought.

It was—except, after his first term, the program went bankrupt and Jeff was back at our college. A sympathetic dean supported him in designing an independent major in community and technology, mingling economics, urban sociology, engineering, internships on wind and solar energy, and as many exchange courses at the nearby art school they would allow.

Jeff graduated in the middle of the Carter years, a golden age for inner-city social projects, and he soon wound up at a place called the Center for Community Technology, working with out-of-school teenagers on alternative energy systems and construction. But then Reagan was elected, the Stockman budget passed, and the plug was pulled on the program. The kids were back on the streets and Jeff hitched up to Vermont to play his guitar and lick his wounds.

There he fell in with a bunch of creative, committed activist architects. Under their influence, he was soon off to the University of New Mexico, enrolled in their master's program in architecture. Within two years he'd taken every energy course they had, while also working for the state to solar-retrofit rural Indian settlements. He transferred to the University of Oregon, truly mecca for the study of alternative energy, then finally finished his rather extended education at Columbia, getting a master's in urban design.

Back in Oregon, he became a practicing architect and started a project that demonstrated how to recycle construction materials from old buildings, an effort that turned into a national and international phenomenon. As a result, he was hired away from his own company by a big firm that wanted to start a "green architecture" division. Next stop: Portland's Bureau of Planning, where within a year or so he was the senior urban designer of America's model city.

A lot of guys my age still have the ponytail and the earring, but not that many still have the politics to go with it. Jeff has them all: he's gone from being one of the country's most fingerprinted undergraduates to working inside the system in a powerful way.

That's what you can do if you never give up.

When I was talking to Michael Nye about my idea of never abandoning the thing you care about most, he pointed out that for most people, this isn't the problem. The problem is figuring out what they care about at all. They don't know what they want to do. Even bright, creative people can find themselves lost and tortured when it comes to finding their way in the world of work and activity.

Michael's suggestion, and it was such a good one that he should probably write his own advice book, was, "Nurture your curiosity." You read, you reflect, you ask other people questions—and you pay close attention to what they say. You listen to music, watch movies, look at art and magazines and Web sites. You leave the house; you travel and see the world. You keep your antennae up. As Michael put it, you see what resonates on the surface of your skin.

When something does, chase it down and spend some time with it. Don't let it get away from you. Find out more.

Write down every interesting idea you have.

If somebody compliments you on something, don't just dismiss it. Think about what it means that you are good at that, or have that quality. What else could you do with it? Hey, I wrote this whole book because the students at Ocean Township liked my talk so much that night.

Take yourself seriously. If you've got a fantasy of building a computer or attending a summer writing conference or selling lava lamps at flea markets, figure out what it would take to accomplish that and take a step in that direction.

Find people who are living lives you admire. Get in touch with them, as Michael did. Ask them questions. Hang out with them. See what they're actually doing every day.

Don't give up on pursuits that don't bear fruit immediately.

Pursue whims. Act on hunches. Remember dreams.

Think twice before saying no to any request or opportunity.

Don't be discouraged if you don't end up with the lofty career in the arts you once imagined; this is not the be-all and end-all of existence. Don't let your failure to be Georgia O'Keeffe or Mozart cause you to give up altogether. Even if you are not the best whatever-it-is in the world, you can still derive great joy from it and give pleasure to others with your talent and skill. Somebody writes the columns in the local paper. Somebody acts in the summer musical. Somebody gets to paint a jungle mural on the wall of your

139

dining room, and rock bands can survive and thrive at many levels, from let's-just-get-together-and-jam to local gigs and independently produced CDs. Without all the twinkling stars in the heavens, the night would be dark indeed.

Never stop looking around. Nurturing your curiosity is an ongoing process, because even once you settle on something, you will always need new information. If you write, you'll need to know what to write about. If you make things, you need to know what to make. And there's always the possibility that you'll find a whole new love: the way Michael found photography, the way I found running, the way Morgan found macrobiotics, the way my mother found on-line bridge.

Michael told me that when he was seven years old in the Gulf coast town of Corpus Christi, he noticed a photograph in the local paper. It was a family seeing the ocean for the first time. The thing was, they lived only forty miles away from the shore.

"At first I thought they were idiots," Michael explained, "but after I tacked the photo up over my desk for a while, I started to see it differently. I realized we're all like that. We all have an ocean forty miles away that we've never seen."

6

Learn to use a semicolon

When people glance over my seven things, this is the one that seems to stop them in their tracks. What can I possibly mean? How could learning to use a semicolon be one of the secrets of life? While the other rules don't tend to draw much argument, the only people who nod and smile at this one are English teachers.

Well, I really do mean learn to use a semicolon, both because I have a deep-seated love of punctuation marks and because I believe that everyone should learn to write competently. But I also mean this metaphorically. Even the most creative endeavors require something more than inspiration and enthusiasm, I've learned. They demand craft and skill. Even if you intend to break the rules, you first have to know what they are. When visiting an exhibition of children's drawings, Picasso remarked, "When I was their age, I could draw like Raphael, but it took me a lifetime to learn to draw like them." True freedom is not ignorant of structure; it absorbs and surpasses it.

In addition to a mastery of craft and a knowledge of the rules, every creative endeavor also requires diligence and discipline. While most of us have heard the standard formulations—Edison's "genius": 1 percent inspiration, 99 percent perspiration; Woody Allen's "success": 80 percent showing up—the romantic image of the dissolute artist still exerts a powerful hold. Well, I've tried both approaches, so I can tell you a little about how they've worked for me.

One of the ways Crispin and I knew we were meant for each other was that we both had the same intense feelings about punctuation. So strongly did we respond to the flavor and rhythm of these little pinpricks and curlicues of ink that we could have long conversations analyzing them, as if they were political movements or films. We both loved the sturdy semicolon, braced to hold a full sentence on either side. A deep connection to the semicolon, we agreed, is the mark of a punctuation connoisseur. Ellipses we scorned, using them rarely and ironically, and we both abhorred the abuse of scare quotes. Today, for example, we saw a utility truck that purported to be "PROFESSIONALLY DRIVEN." Exactly what did they mean by those quotation marks? We wondered if we should just pull over and let him go by.

While we shared a persnickety standard for usage and

spelling and would go purse lipped and horrified over typos and other errors in the newspaper, we each also had a bit of the maverick in us. Each had blazed ahead to pioneer alternate punctuation forms, things that might seem wrong to others but to us were a kind of silent poetry within the sentence, as well as a more efficient and accurate infrastructure to convey the sense of the words they shouldered along.

Crispin's major innovation is the use of multiple colons in one sentence. For him, this creates a kind of egalitarian community among thoughts: a way of interconnecting ideas without subordinating one to the other: a continuous system for sending out explanations one after the next, like waves lapping up on the shore. It's more than a mannerism: colons actually help him think. And while he does understand why the editors of his newspaper articles and books invariably force him to reduce all sentences to one colon or less each, these unanesthetized colostomies have to hurt.

I know how he feels. The first time I had an article accepted for publication—it was called "How to Get Pregnant in the Modern World," and it appeared in the *Austin Chronicle*—I was shocked and enraged to see they had corrected my punctuation. I wrote a long single-spaced letter to the editor explaining just how much time I had spent making those mistakes, and how deeply I cared about them. I was a poet, for God's sake, or at least I used to be, and as such did not feel I was limited by the petty maunderings of the *Chicago Manual of Style.*

The editor thought I was out of my mind, and also he thought I was wrong. However, since they were paying me so very little and since they were a groovy alternative newspaper and not an official organ of the plutocracy, they thereafter allowed me to come down to the office and review the galleys of my typeset articles, clothespinned to a string in the hall on the way to pasteup. Every week, the long-suffering copy editor / rock-and-roll guitarist Mike Hall listened to my ravings, explained once again why we would be punctuating the sentence the way normal people do, and sent me on my way.

(On the other hand, the *Chronicle* did let me use really bad four-letter words in my articles on occasion without a peep, most notably in an interview with the writer Bret Easton Ellis, the guy who wrote *Less Than Zero* and *American Psycho.* I was trying to find out whether this dude was gay or bi or what, and finally, to the shock of his publicist and my boyfriend, who were in the car with us at the time, I just asked him some extremely blunt questions phrased in exceptionally graphic language. I included my questions and his answers in my piece and they printed it word for word. I loved them for it.)

Though I have had no more luck than Crispin in getting my punctuation innovations into print, I still have a weakness for the occasional intentional comma fault. In my case, the aberration arises from an attempt to make my sentences echo not my thoughts but my voice. As much as I love a semicolon, they never seem right for indicating the way two sentences are adjoined when I say them aloud. Like when I say, "Fuck them, it's just you and me talking here." See, it should be, "Fuck them; it's just you and me talking here," but doesn't that just seem wrong? There's another thing I like—dialogue without quotes—and sometimes I even do questions without question marks. I like the way it flattens the affect of the spoken words, blurs the distinction between what is thought and what is said in a kind of hip, understated way.

These poor, poor people, you must be thinking. Have they no lives? And you also may be thinking that for a chapter that purports to deal with learning to use a semicolon, we certainly have spent a lot of time talking about breaking the rules.

But you can't break the rules until you know what they are, nor can you make jokes about them, subvert them, or reinterpret them. And sometimes you'll simply want to follow them. For even if you are not a writer, your writing is a mirror of yourself. Throughout your life, people will judge how smart you are by the way you express yourself on paper, or on a computer screen perhaps. While nobody expects perfection in an instant message between friends, a letter or e-mail about a job opportunity is another story. The point is to make your writing as smart as you are. It may take some heavy lifting in the apostrophe gym, but you can do it.

The other thing I should say about our love of punctuation marks is that they are a symbol of commitment to craft, of our sense of language as something we make things out of, like clay or wool or wood, and our joy in the process of that making, even the parts of it that seem tedious or mundane.

Inspiration is good. It is important. But craft and diligence and discipline are just as important. I think probably more so, in the long run, at least if you ever want to get anything done.

I did not always see it this way. In fact, I was long under the impression that the great works of literature were written at two in the morning on cocktail napkins in smoky bars, generally by drunken geniuses garbed in black. Since

I was then trying to write poetry, which tends to be cocktail napkin in size, at least, this approach actually worked for me for a while.

I started writing poetry as a way to express intense emotions, and since throughout my adolescence I was frequently beset by such emotions, I was quite the prolific little miss. By the time I was in my early twenties, though, I had run into a couple of problems with my system. For one thing, I had begun to go through longer periods without having an idea, or at least an idea I or someone else hadn't already had. Since I believed I had no control of this process, there was nothing I could do about it. Nothing except fret and complain, which I did until even I could not stand it anymore.

The other difficulty with my creative process was finding the exact level of drunkenness that would lead to good cocktail napkin composition. If I remembered to write anything at all after drinking the bottle of wine it might just be indecipherable, or if I could decipher anything it would turn out to say, "The dark birds in the hollow of your cheek," or, "Dream of the perfect circle," and I would have no idea what I meant to do with it. Even more often I would lose the cocktail napkin, or wash it in my pants. Believing groundlessly that this napkin contained the priceless germ of my greatest work ever, I would devote hours and hours to looking for it and grieving over its disappearance. Attempting to assuage the pain with a glass or two of, say, ice-cold Stoli, I might scribble some words about my loss on a second cocktail napkin and begin the process again. Alternately, I would take drugs instead of drink, in which case the idea would never even make it to the napkin phase and I would spend days trying to remember the great idea, which was something about birds, or was it?

Amazingly, I thought of this whole process as "writing."

Since waiting to be assaulted by ideas and allotting no time whatsoever to nurturing, cultivating, or exploring them in any systematic way did pay off for me for a while, when it stopped working I was pissed. I was so pissed that, as I explained earlier, I announced to everyone that I had quit writing, had given up my great ambition in life, would have to find some other way to live, because I simply had no ideas and couldn't stand the frustration anymore.

Shortly after my retirement from creative writing I met Morgan Jones and convinced him to give me a job at his software company as a "documentalist," which he explained in his charming Texas way meant producing the documentation for the company's software programs. Though I was soon to be spending eight or more hours every day sitting at a computer typing—pages, chapters, books, and multivolume sets—I didn't realize at first that I had in fact gotten a job as a writer. What I did realize is that I knew almost nothing about computers, and I wanted to. It was 1983: there was no such thing as a Mac, no Windows, no accessible Internet, nada. Though I had no sense of how prevalent and cool and essential computers were about to become, I did have the feeling that this was a new and enticing world, not much like the one I'd explored in our high school class in Fortran, when we keyed in our computer programs on punch cards.

Not only was writing computer manuals different from anything I'd done before, they were paying more money for it than anything I'd done. As a liberal arts graduate, I was shocked and thrilled to learn I had any marketable skill whatsoever. Tech writers, it seemed, made real money. On the other hand, this is how I knew for sure it couldn't be anything hip or creative or even what I thought of as writing, since no one would possibly pay me for that. Real artists starved in garrets, worked as waiters, or applied for grants to support their projects. Since I had already done all of those with poor results—I was fired from my waitress job while still in training—I was ready to try something with some zeros in the salary.

Since Morgan Jones's company made utility software for the HP 3000 business computer system, my job was a crash course for me in some rather arcane topics: system backup, terminal emulation, parallel processing, and C compilers, to name a few. But learning so many new things was exciting. I had entered that post-compulsory-education phase where you start to see what a privilege and what fun learning is—when you realize it is actually like traveling, or meeting new people, or taking psychedelic drugs: a way of changing your head and your life. Also, I loved being around the programmers. They were so smart and logical and unpretentious, and boy, had they learned to use a semicolon—one at the end of every line of the hundreds of lines of code they churned out every day. They had no illusions that you could make something without nuts and bolts, or without long hours of hard work. Their most outlandish and inventive solutions were only as good as the routines that carried them out.

By the third year of this job, I started to get the urge to write my own stuff again. The process didn't seem so mysterious anymore, and it had nothing to do with cocktail napkins. It was now clear to me that if you sat yourself down in front of a keyboard every day, you would eventually type things, and these things would become articles and books and such. I got a little Macintosh and started typing at home evenings and weekends. And basically have not stopped since.

The Israeli novelist Amos Oz said something about writing I've had tacked up over my desk for a long time. "Let me just say that I'm a very steady worker," he told an interviewer from the *New York Times*. "After my desert walk, I read through the newspapers, several of them—a religious duty of sorts for most Israelis—then I try to write for a few hours. Sometimes this is a source of frustration—if nothing happens. When I lived on the kibbutz, this could make me feel terribly guilty. I'd come to the communal dining hall for lunch, look at all the people who'd been plowing the land, milking cows, and driving tractors for the whole morning, and I'd feel as if I hadn't really earned my lunch. Over the years I've developed the self-image of a shopkeeper. Mainly, it is my business to open the joint at a set time, to sit and wait. If I have customers, it's a blessed day. If I don't, well, I'm still doing my job."

If you don't open the shop, if you expect the customers to track you down at home in front of the TV or ambush you in a bar at 3 A.M., well, don't be surprised if you don't get many. For me, this open-the-shop attitude changed everything. Once I sat down and started typing, I had more ideas than I knew what to do with. I found that a very small idea can often be coaxed into something lovely, or funny, or surprising, and sometimes a big idea folds itself up and hides inside a small one. It's not that you do without inspiration altogether—it's that you go out and meet it halfway. And you meet it with a keyboard under your fingers or pencil and paper in your hand, rather than a shot of tequila and a cigarette. The extremely prolific comedian Steve Allen once explained that he didn't have any more ideas than most people, he just wrote them down and used them.

A few years back, I spent a couple of weeks at an artists' colony in the foothills of the Smoky Mountains. This was the first time I was really exposed to the work habits of visual artists. I was as impressed as I had been by computer programmers. These people were putting in eighteen-hour days, preparing canvases, firing kilns, stringing looms, mixing chemicals, and focusing enlargers. There was no question of waiting around for the magic. They had work to do. If you saw them for an hour at dinner you were lucky, and most of them would jump right up afterward to get back to their studios.

This was quite different from most of the writers I had known. If you got a bunch of us gasbags together at a place like this, dinner would be a multihour affair. We would sit around drinking coffee until it was time to switch to booze and then back again, talking, talking, talking. Even the quieter ones would stay on, listening. Their verbal skills and interest in people tended to keep many of the writers I'd met tied up far from their desks, and while I knew they were writing sometime, somewhere, since they had finished works to prove it, I never saw how or when or got much of an example I could follow.

I wanted to be like these visual artists, industriously buzzing all day. One problem I ran into is that writing has less busywork in it than other arts and pursuits. I didn't have something mindless and soothing to do, like sanding my planks or carding my skeins or mixing my colors. Most of writing required full-bore attention and creative engagement, and since I couldn't do that for eight hours a day or even close to it, I started to learn to use my other time to do things that supported the process, like reading or watching movies or going for walks. If I couldn't get anywhere on the main thing I was working on, I might try something else: a poem, or a letter to a friend, or a book review. And it's not that I did it for eighteen hours. But I certainly no longer expected it to take eighteen minutes.

If you have an addictive personality, as I do, you can actually put it to work for you in accomplishing your goals. I have seen this most clearly in the realm of exercise, which I came to rather late in life, when I had already learned a lot about what motivates me to do things.

In my youth, I had a kind of positive commitment to avoiding exercise, a slacker aesthetic. I was a freak, not a jock. The only ball I played was pinball and I went to stadiums only for rock concerts. Eventually, all that changed.

I guess I was experiencing that midlife urge to get in shape at least once before you cash it in altogether. Also, I wanted to go outside. Adult life seemed kind of cooped up. But when I first started trying to run, I could not go a half mile, and my pace was so slow, it could not even be called jogging—it was more like "hurrying." I had a long way to go. I knew I wasn't going to get there by telling myself it was good for me, or that I should. Self-flagellation (You're fat! You're bad! You're lazy!) has never panned out for me either. If I did it, it would have to be because it felt good, or bad in a good way, like getting a tattoo. Or because I was selfish and it was a way to escape from the chores and the kids and the house and the ringing phone. If I was going to make exercise a habit, it would have to be something like a drug habit: an exquisite, irresistible mix of guilt and desire.

Even after I had my unique form of self-discipline in place, I found I was still not very good at running. And this was just fine. It completely freed me from competitiveness, from comparing myself to others and struggling to improve. It's hopeless, and it isn't the point. If I sign up for a race, it's only to be there. I just smile and wave as the five or six thousand people run past me. Finally, those old East-ern philosophical principles in action!

Exercise turned out to be a mental challenge more than a physical one. It is all about what you have decided you can do. The muscle you stretch most thoroughly is your will, and just as the physical fitness you get spills over into other areas of life, so does the tough-mindedness. I run because it makes me feel I can do anything.

There is always a moment of resistance or inertia at the beginning of every activity, when you don't want to do it. You don't want to exercise. You don't want to write. You don't want to leave on the journey, or even get ready for the party. This one moment is what will is for. Then the hardest part is over. Inertia's on your side now; the rest is just coasting.

Whether it's writing or running or some other discipline, I've learned to stick by certain rules. I do it when I say I'm going to do it, and I go as far as I said I would. I don't break my promises to myself. If it's a big project, I divide it into little pieces: A book of fifty thousand words can be written a thousand words at a time in a couple of months. Twenty miles a week is four five-mile runs.

I enjoy where I'm at, take pleasure in what I've done. I give myself good equipment and treats as necessary. I have learned to lean on and value the structure these endeavors give to my life, the meaning, the orderliness. When I have to make choices, I know what my priorities are. Self-discipline, in my experience, pays off in self-esteem and self-sufficiency.

I seem to have come a long way from the cocktail napkins.

Nothing is as black-and-white as you think it is. The things that seem to be strictly for Goody Two-Shoes, like grammar and physical fitness and diligence and saving money, can just as easily be part of the arsenal of the artiste. There is a stage in life when appearances are more important than substance, when you care more about shaping how you live and how you are perceived than actually doing or creating anything in particular. What you are making, at this point, is your image. This is fine, but it is a stage you will have to outgrow and be done with if you plan to go on to other projects. Because just looking the way you think an artist should look or acting the way you think an artist acts won't get any art done (for artist you can substitute playwright, computer genius, musician, even millionaire). First you have to sit down and do something. Then an artist will look like you.

The most important habits you can develop are ones

that keep you alive and well and able to work. Self-destructiveness has been associated with the creative personality from Vincent van Gogh to Kurt Cobain, and drinking, in particular, with writers. It once seemed you had to be a drunk to be a writer: all the best writers were (Fitzgerald, O'Neill, Faulkner, Hemingway, Tennessee Williams, Carson McCullers, Dorothy Parker, Dylan Thomas, and Edna St. Vincent Millay, to name just a few). But none of them were still doing good work by the time they reached middle age, if they reached it at all.

Today's writers, from John Irving to Mary Karr, from Stephen King to Anne Lamott, will probably be laboring productively into their discount-at-the-movies years since so many of them are recovered alcoholics or some other version of determined nondrinker. With so many excellent examples before us, I think more people are figuring out ahead of time that raging alcoholism does not equal creative genius. We really don't have to conduct the experiments ourselves. Attempts at artistic expression that involve drug addiction and suicide attempts typically end badly as well.

But this is not to say you can't have any fun in life. The other traditional bohemian pursuits, like staying up nights in bars or cafés, listening to music, drinking wine, and smoking cigarettes, going to parties that never end with people who never shut up, traveling with no money, kissing with no promises, dressing with no underwear, writing with no punctuation—Lord knows I have loved them all. I would never begrudge anyone his or her dissolution, messiness, decadence, and chaos. As long as you don't let them get the better of you, those things can have their place in a well-rounded biography.

But eventually you do want to do things, and if you try to do them while keeping up a host of self-indulgent, self-destructive, or even just unhealthful habits, you'll eventually find you've gotten work done in spite of these habits and not because of them. And there will be a time when you have to choose between these habits and quieter, more nourishing ones, and I hope you choose to open the shop.

My favorite sight in all of nature is the sunrise over the ocean. When I was a teenager, my friends and I would go down the beach to watch it at the end of a long night doing who-knows-what. Now I get up in the dark to see it at the beginning of the day with my bright-eyed baby in my lap. It was beautiful then; it is beautiful now, and just as refreshing to the soul.

Note the correct use of the semicolon.

you wiLL fiND Love

Readers, there is none of you more desperate than I was, none of you more lonely and horny and crazed! If there's a miracle in this book, it is in this chapter. Here I tell you about my oversexed and underloved ways, and all the trouble I got in before I finally understood: you can't force it, you gotta trust it, and you have to treat it with tenderness and care when it finally arrives. Then I've got some real-life love stories, just to show how tricky and various this thing really is.

Well, it turns out this is it: the thing I know now that I most wish I could have known then. Because when I look back I see that loneliness, frustrated passion, and doubts about my lovability were behind most of the worst decisions I made in my life, from my sad little Excedrin-overdose "suicide attempt" in seventh grade to many other embarrassing, stupid, and sometimes disastrous attempts to get attention and be fascinating and irresistible—the worst of which led to my getting pregnant in the fall of my senior year of high school.

I felt a kind of desperation and urgency about finding love that I know now is a least common denominator for most people, fueled by hormones and cultural myths and various mysteries of the psyche. But back then it felt like it was me alone. Ironically, my neediness was something that isolated me from other people rather than helped me connect with them. It made me kind of scary; I was often described as "too intense." (Admittedly, I am still described as intense. But usually not "too" intense.) And I think now I wasn't all that much scarier than other people, just far less skilled at hiding it, and that in my desperation I was seriously confused. Ah, let me count the ways.

I confused sex with love.

I confused like with love.

I confused infatuation with love.

I confused need with love.

By the time I was twenty-three years old and met my first husband, Tony, I was very, very unhappy and self-destructive. If drugs and alcohol were the way I acted it out, its cause was a sense of worthlessness, ugliness, and despair about ever being cared for the way I so frantically needed to be. I was at my all-time peak of recklessness and carelessness, throwing myself into this or that experience or this or that bed, not to feel but to stop feeling. To bury my rawness and pain under a thick layer of cynicism and bitterness.

I can't imagine what it would have been like if I could have seen into a crystal ball, seen how well I would be loved. That I would have an amazing marriage to an amazing person and that after he died, young and tragically, destiny would bring me another soul mate to share my life with. That I would have children, and get to know how being a mother changes absolutely everything, connecting us to the world with a bond deeper than blood. I wish I could have known that I couldn't have the kind of love I wanted until I finished growing up, and that I could let that process unfold a little more gradually.

So though I don't know whether my saying this can help anyone else, I want to try. I want to say: Give it time and you will get all the love you need. Even more important, you will get to give all the love you can. You will create as many outlets for love as you have love to fill them. If you have to have four cats, five kids, six best friends, and an intense, passionate marriage, like me, just to start finding a place to put all the energy of your emotions, you will. And if, on the other hand, you need a lot of space, a lot of time alone, and maybe just a dog and an occasional date, you'll create that situation instead. (As Crispin, the aforementioned

Hermit Boy, puts it: no matter how you hide, love will find you—and drive you out of your mind.)

Love and work are the two things that fit us into the world, that tell us where and how we belong. They are the web we spin to hold us in place. We come in, if we're lucky, with some love given: the love of our parents and family. And then we get to have friends. And then we learn about the magic of the twosome, and the even more dizzying power of romance. For me, it seemed like everything: a religion, a drug, a reason to live.

I always believed in love, always thought it was the most important thing. Since the day I could cut the shape of a heart from a piece of red construction paper, I fell in love, I fell in love, I fell and fell until I hit the bottom, the hard and rocky bottom of the pit of rejection. There I languished for an appropriate interval of mourning, then picked myself up, dusted myself off, and rushed headlong to the flame again. No matter how often my heart was broken, I never stopped; I was virtually addicted to the state of infatuation, that headlong tumble through nothing-else-exists euphoria. My capacity for pain was equaled only by my capacity for bliss.

As a girl and then a young woman with a romantic streak a mile wide, I was on a constant quest for the perfect experience of emotional love. Once my teenage libido kicked in,

I was equally intrigued by the physical aspects. And while it all started out pretty icky and confusing and not the way I expected (what were you supposed to *feel* when they stuck their hand up your shirt? I was sure it wasn't what I was feeling at all), by the time I was fifteen I had a really sweet boyfriend and a copy of *The Sensuous Woman,* and the sexual revolution was under way in my very own garage.

And in bathrooms at parties, at the matinee of the new Brooke Shields movie—just about anywhere my boyfriend and I could be alone or at least in the dark. But even with our enthusiasm, it took us half a year to master the actual sex act. It really hurt, and my lover was a gentle type. It got to the point where we'd come downstairs after a few hours in his bedroom to join our friends who'd been hanging out in the living room. They'd all look up and say, "Well, did you do it?" We'd look at each other, unsure.

"If you're not sure, you didn't do it," they told us.

Finally, one February evening, we decided we had done it. We celebrated our success with our entire entourage over cheeseburgers. Everyone was so happy for us. Or at least glad it was over.

After this sweetie pie and I went our separate ways, I was hooked on the sex-and-love combination, but I kept going at it from the sex side. I thought you could be attracted to someone, seduce them, sleep with them, and go straight back to the love heaven I had had before. It seemed to me that sex created love, or at least entailed it. In fact, it proved to be quite the opposite, and it was a long while before I matched my idyllic first experience again. I learned the hard way, through rejection and disappointment, that sex doesn't necessarily have anything to do with love, that just because somebody "makes love" to you doesn't mean he cares about you at all. Sex can generate distance, can cause pain, can produce an experience of isolation all the more bitter for the fantasy of closeness and the reality of physical contact that produces it. To touch the skin without ever touching the heart: I wouldn't have dreamed it was possible, but it was actually quite common.

Like most adolescent girls, I was convinced that I was fat and ugly. There was no part of me, to be honest, that I liked. Despite years and years of dieting that eventually resulted in a kind of bizarre involuntary bulimia, I did not look like Susan Dey on *The Partridge Family* or the captain of the cheerleading squad. And even though my mother informed me in advance that this was not true, I thought sex could make me feel pretty. If I could pick out some attractive, ultracool guy and get him to make love to me, how ugly could I be? Those precious moments of total attention, of closeness and passion, of what seemed like love, drew me like a moth to the flame.

And I use the old cliché advisedly, because I definitely got burned. After the good part came the bad part, when what seemed like love turned out to be idle recreation, and my silly heart was broken all over again. Many of the heart-breakers were basically worthless hoods who spent my money and had me clean their apartments and bail them out of jail, but the one that hurt me the deepest, the one who still pops up in dreams twenty-five years later, was not in this category. He was a smart, funny, moody, curly-haired boy in my honors calculus class, and I was crazy about him. I did anything to be with him, joined clubs at school I had no interest in, watched sports on TV, became a drug dealer so he'd have to call me when he ran out of pot. I thought that if he knew me and understood me and wanted me, my troubles would be over for life.

Despite the fact that I soon deduced that he was more interested in Sandye, of course, who couldn't have cared less about him, I wanted to be with this boy more than any-thing else in life. I engineered situation after situation to seduce him and finally managed it, a short-lived drunken interlude that left its trace not in his heart but in my uterus. Meanwhile, he had come down with some kind of STD, which I was sure I had nothing to do with and he was equally convinced I had. It was a terrible, sordid mess for both of us.

My parents paid for the abortion. I felt so humiliated, so ashamed, and so wrong.

Not long after this I entered my Hindu phase and gave up sex altogether, but no matter how much I meditated, read books about spirituality and psychology, visited the psychiatrists my parents sent me to, and tried to transcend my stupid obsessive neediness, I really never succeeded in stopping the hypnotic trance of attraction from taking over my body and brain on a regular basis. But I had begun to see that what I craved was not sex itself (or to be honest, not *just* sex itself) but the way it gets you closer to another person than almost anything else, the way it dissolves boundaries and takes you past any consciousness of self. The roles that can be played in bed, the intensity and vulnerability that can be expressed, are just not possible in any other type of interaction. And though I tried to protect myself, my romantic nature often pushed me over the line.

No matter how I tried to deny it, ignore it, or work around it, I finally had to admit that to love someone physically without at least beginning to love them emotionally was virtually impossible for me—unless I was drunk or on drugs, which I often was. It took me a long time to quit trying to fight or drown that urge. I was a grown woman before I believed that I could have a relationship that was about sex and love equally, where I could express all the passion

inside me and feel it returned, where I didn't have to protect myself, where I could just keep opening doors. I
couldn't settle for less again.

I don't regret my past in the sense that I judge myself.
But I regret the amount I suffered and the time and energy
I wasted. One thing it took me about thirty years to figure
out is that when someone is right for you, they will know it
too. Maybe not the first second, maybe not as soon as you
do, but soon. That is where the magic lies, and it is a magic
that cannot be coerced.

Sex means different things to different people. Sandye,
for instance, has always had a different attitude than I.
While both of us had quite a busy period in the boy department, Sandye was more the bohemian New York artist with
the unconventional love life, whereas I was more the ongoing train wreck.

Sandye's first great love was in art school, and it ended
badly shortly after graduation. Perhaps she didn't believe,
deep down, that Jim loved her and would make a life with
her, and that's what made it okay in her head to drift away
from him. Perhaps she did believe it, at least part of the
time, and that was just as scary and distancing. Perhaps
the beginning of our heavy vodka-and-quaalude years had
something to do with it, too. But in any case, after it hap-

pened and hearts were broken, she decided not to make any more promises for a long time. In fact, this period lasted twenty years.

Sandye wanted to go out with men and she wanted to have sex and she felt that love wasn't necessarily required for those things. She had no double standard: you couldn't ask her to make promises, but she didn't care what you were doing when you weren't with her, either. As I pointed out earlier, she is quite a good-looking girl and with these factors combined, she had as many men as she could handle; some stopped in for an evening, others hung around for years. Some of them she thought were really adorable, and several wanted a more serious relationship, but she had learned that the safest thing was to keep it breezy and not let the situation get out of hand. (And, she adds, if she wasn't your girlfriend, she didn't have to pick up your socks and wash your dishes—aspects of couplehood she was never that enthused about.)

Deep down, Sandye did want true love with just one other person, but perhaps because she had little hope of finding it, she settled for keeping busy and having fun. Being in charge of her love life in this way made her feel independent, powerful, and secure—and kept her from taking risks that might not have worked out.

Finally, one of these casual interests proved passionate

and intense and persistent enough to become a major full-time boyfriend—and to Sandye's utter shock, he turned out to be an absolute nightmare from hell. After spending almost two years with this alcoholic junkie kleptomaniac, this abusive, violent "surrealist poet," Sandye was in really bad shape. Though she'd quit drinking while living with him, after she finally got him out (with the help of the New York Police Department), she returned to Mr. Jack Daniel with a vengeance. This resulted in a dark period that culminated in another spectacularly bad choice, this time with a more amiable roaring drunk—he literally roared, bellowing in restaurants, hollering at parties, swigging back whole bottles of hooch—though he was a pretty nice guy who made charming prints and paintings.

Sandye returned to the multiman love style after she got rid of the roarer, but I believe with less zest than before. We were getting older; she wanted a quieter life. By now, she'd almost given up on having a baby. But then, out of the last crop of musicians and performance artists emerged a guy she'd fallen for hard fifteen years earlier, right when she moved to New York after college. Things hadn't worked out at the time but the chemistry had always been there when their paths crossed.

Running into each other over the years, they became something like friends. Then a couple of years ago, the friendship deepened. Rik, who had given up drugs and alcohol six years earlier, stood by Sandye as she made those changes herself—and soon the no-strings-attached girl was living with a man, and going into business ventures with him, and then having their baby.

Still, no marriage for Sandye: she hates government, religion, and bureaucracy, and to her, the institution of marriage is the evil spawn of all three. She says that when she thinks of marrying even someone she loves, she feels like she can't breathe. But she has the commitment and the depth of feeling that for most of us is the essence of marriage anyway.

As hard as I looked for love, Sandye hid from it as carefully as she could. But it found her in the end, too.

It found Michael Nye a little more easily. He was twenty-eight years old, one year out of law school, working in San Antonio at Appellate Court. One day a friend from work told him and another guy to come along to lunch; she was meeting a girl named Naomi Shihab. You'll like her, she said.

When Naomi arrived at the cafe, she learned that her friend had invited these two other lawyers to share their table. Looking up at Michael, she realized with certainty that he was the man she would marry. She was suddenly very glad she had come to this lunch.

There was just one problem. She had determined once and for all only the day before to stop thinking of men altogether—to live singly, with great concentration and focus, doing her writing and working with kids. Having flipped back and forth among many halfhearted, confusing relationships in the preceding months, having said no to a number of proposals, she had taken a vow of autonomy. It lasted twenty-four hours. The day she met Michael, she told a friend she would marry him and even sent a letter to her parents telling them about it.

Michael did not get a similar telegram from destiny at lunch that day, but he did think the woman across the table was one of the most alive, electric people he had ever met. And she was in the arts! She wrote poetry and music! She loved to travel and seemed completely in charge of her own life! He was captivated and charmed, as are most people who have met Naomi before or since.

Naomi invited the whole lunch group to dinner at her house the following evening, saying they could bring anyone they wanted, secretly hoping to find out if Michael had a wife or girlfriend. He brought his slides of Guatemala.

She waited for him to make the next move. It took three months. At this point, marriage was far from Michael's thoughts. He was not attracted to a traditional life, in terms of a wife and kids and regular job hours. He had a number of casual girlfriends and female chums but enjoyed playing tennis or reading philosophy about as much as dating. Yet eventually, he found himself dialing Naomi's number, and shortly thereafter his dating schedule condensed.

She had not been thinking of marrying a lawyer. He was not thinking of a poet/songwriter, or of settling down at all. But about a year from the time they met, he went away to visit an uncle who was dying. On that trip, he thought about what it would be like to have a life with Naomi. Then he thought about what it would be like to have a life without her.

After that, they got married.

The lucky ducks.

Kathryn Korniloff was fourteen years old the day her mom looked up from an article in the newspaper and posed a question that changed the shape of the world. "Did you know Janis Ian was bisexual?" her mother asked.

Korn had never heard the word before but she knew immediately that it was very important. As her mother explained what it meant, and about homo- and heterosexuality, she was filled with both joy and despair. It was great that there were words for it, this thing she had felt even when she was eleven or twelve and absolutely sure she would never marry or have children. But, oh my God, if she *was* one—if she was part of this fringe group of people, this thing that was definitely not okay, that her mother could never approve of . . . shit!

All through her teen years, Korn dated boys. In junior high, she was part of an avant-garde cadre that smoked pot, wore Earth shoes, made out, and streaked around town (sorry, it was the seventies, what can I say?). She had one really serious relationship with a boy she met sophomore year while her family was living in Holland. He courted her practically in her hospital bed, where she lay recovering from the open-heart surgery she'd had to correct a congenital defect, then continued his attentions from afar after he started college in New York.

After her father's sudden death—this was the year from hell for Korn—she and her mom moved back to El Paso. Her boyfriend planned to come down for the summer, but in the meantime she made friends with the weirdos in town. She and her new gang, particularly one skinny, red-headed, gay-and-no-way-to-hide-it boy, were determined to find the underground, cool part of El Paso that they were sure was there somewhere.

Finally they dug up a little art-house cinema with a pool table and a bar. One night the theater screened a very explicit lesbian silent movie. Korn was practically vibrating as she watched it, and soon afterward she found herself doing strange things. Like trying to subtly convince her boyfriend not to transfer to the University of Texas at Austin, where she would matriculate in the fall. Like hanging around the auto parts department of Sears, where the really masculine woman who worked at the counter filled her with fascination. The taboo, the fear, the sense that she might be part of a secret elite that had renounced tradition and mediocrity for something far more exciting—these were an intoxicating brew.

After his summer visit, her boyfriend left for school in Austin and Korn set out to make good use of the two weeks until she joined him. Night after night at happy hour, she went down to a seedy gay club that she and her friends had found, sat at the bar, and waited for something to happen.

"Wait till you get to Austin," the bartender advised her. "This is no kind of place."

But something did happen. One night a beautiful woman walked in and asked her to dance. They closed down the bar that night and made plans to meet again, when the woman came back into town from her home in Las Cruces, New Mexico. Korn was a wreck. She had never felt more terrified, or more alive.

She needed to answer the question "Am I a lesbian?"

with a sexual experience, one that might begin to tell her why she felt like such an outsider. And while her night in the shag-carpeted van of the woman from Las Cruces did give her some useful information about how her body responded, this woman, who turned out to be both alcoholic and married—she and her husband shared the van for these forays to El Paso—couldn't tell her all she needed to know about who she was, and what it meant to be that way.

When she told her boyfriend simply, "I like girls," he thought she was kidding. But she wasn't. And the bartender was right—at U.T. there was a feminist bookstore, and a Women's Center, and a bunch of lesbians her age just waiting to become friends. There was also a separatist feminist Marxist alcoholic from Abilene ready to snap her up and provide her first experience in what Korn calls "dyke drama." And so the quest for love and self, lesbian style, was on.

Though lovelier times with lovelier women lay ahead, Korn still hasn't settled down for life. Like many lesbians, she's been a serial monogamist, with intense, deeply passionate relationships that lasted eighteen months, two years, four years, seven years—the seven-year ex in particular remains one of the closest people in her life.

One kind of love Korn is particularly rich in is the love of friends. For the gay community (which in Korn's case seems to be the extended ex-girlfriend community), friends are a very real form of family, and in this they are a model for all outsider types, who celebrate birthdays and Thanksgivings together, take care of one another when sick, pick one another up at the airport—having fed one another's pets and stocked one another's refrigerators—and in times of trial, stay on the phone and listen all night long.

Though she's just recovering from an absorbing, heart-wrenching relationship and would still be very interested in Ms. Right, Korn says she has outlived the time when finding a partner is the driving force of her life. The marriage-with-children model of living is increasingly popular with gay people, but she's never been that attracted to it. At this point, she feels it's more important to work on self-acceptance.

There will undoubtedly be many more romances, and perhaps even a big surprise. But the love that has found her through the community of unruly hearts, and through her own growing wisdom, is just as ardently to be sought, and perhaps even more sustaining.

Talk about surprises: let me tell you my favorite love story. It's one where the girl doesn't beat the boy over the head until he finally gives in, and it's about a love that sneaked up on her when she wasn't ready, wasn't looking, was just about ready to settle in for a good two-year cry.

After my husband died, in 1994, I was lucky enough to find a damn fine boyfriend, a divorced guy who was a great cook and had two sweet daughters. We had been dating for almost five years when things started to get a little tense. I knew he thought that after all this time, the next step was getting engaged or at least moving in together. But I was happy the way things were: him in his house, me in mine, each with our own two kids. After the stormy years I'd been through in my marriage, ending with my husband's death, I was afraid to try again. As I told my boyfriend one night at the Rock 'n' Bowl in New Orleans, after a couple of drinks, "I'm so honored that you stick with this relationship despite the fact that I'm not doing what you want me to, and probably never will."

You know, you hear a lot about "Don't drink and drive"; in my case, an equally important warning might be "Don't drink and talk." My boyfriend seemed pensive after hearing this little speech. On the long drive home to Austin the next day, he told me it was over.

"No!" I shouted, but it was too late.

Oh great, Marion, I said to myself. Are you happy now? My fortieth birthday was coming up fast; now I'd be celebrating that milestone alone. I would have to go on blind dates, for God's sake. But first I had to put on some lipstick and pull myself together since my book about the joys of single motherhood was about to be published and I was leaving on a publicity tour.

The first outing was an overnighter to Bel Air, Maryland, a suburb of Baltimore. I was leaving on a Friday morning and coming back the next day. This sounded like a pain to me, but the publicist explained that it would be well worth it. It was School Night at the bookstore, the school orchestra was playing, and "jillions" of parents were expected: a captive audience with credit cards in hand. Giddy, I bought a pair of glamorous Oriental lounging pajamas for the occasion.

I knew something had gone wrong as soon as my driver pulled up in front of the store on the appointed evening. Jillions of parents were there indeed, but they were leaving, struggling to their cars with sleepy children and violin cases. For at least five minutes I couldn't even get in the place due to the throngs pouring out. And by the time I did, about the only people left were two bedraggled employees.

"I'm sorry," one of them said. "School Night ended at seven."

"You're kidding," I said. "That's terrible!"

"Wait, there is one guy here to see you," the clerk remembered, trying to shore up her rapidly disintegrating author. "In fact, he's been here for hours. Go find him, Karen!"

My lone visitor turned out to be a friend of some mutual friends, a philosophy professor / writer guy in a sport coat, running shoes, blond ponytail, and silver earring.

"Thanks for coming," I said, fiddling with a button of what now seemed to be just what they were: bright green fake satin pajamas.

"This must be kind of disappointing for you," he said with concern.

"Oh, heck no," I replied bravely, and to prove it, I insisted on doing a reading for an audience of four: him, the bookstore gals, and my driver. My performance could not have been more gala if I'd been onstage at Kennedy Center, and I'm sure it was that, and not just pity, that motivated all four audience members to buy my book—including the driver, who was from El Salvador and may not have read English.

After I had signed the last grueling autograph, the blue-eyed professor and I went out to dinner. He gave me a copy of his book, titled *Obscenity Anarchy Reality.* Quite a title. Quite a cover, too—it featured a shirtless, well-muscled male torso. Holding the book in my lap at the restaurant, I surreptitiously tried to figure out if the body could be his. Meanwhile, it was turning out we had a lot in common: both writers, both about to turn forty, both single with kids the same ages. We had both been through personal tragedies in which drugs played a nefarious role. But it wasn't just the facts that matched up; it was something more. The click between us was practically audible.

Yet neither of us was thinking of this as the prelude to romance, evidenced by the fact that we spent most of the time discussing our recent breakups. He told me about his new tattoo symbolizing his grief over his young, brilliant ex-fiancée. I would not call this a pickup line. Nonetheless, sometime during dinner, I realized that I was on a date.

At about one in the morning, he left me at my hotel, hugging me good-bye beside his car. And that was all. I was thinking, Wow. If there are guys like this in the world, I'm going to be all right. At least I hoped there were others, because I didn't know if I'd ever see him again.

But the next day when I got home from my pathetic trip, there was an e-mail waiting. It said: "The next time you're in the region, maybe we should sleep in the same bed."

I was dazzled by this directness. "But why didn't you even kiss me when I was sitting there last night five inches away from you?" I typed back.

"Making up for lost time now," said the next message.

After lots of jittery e-mails and phone calls, I arranged

to meet him in Philadelphia, another stop on the book tour. He picked me up at the airport—I felt like a mail order bride getting off that plane—and though we were both almost too nervous to speak, we started to kiss in the parking garage and it was soon clear that everything was going to be fine. (It was definitely him on the book jacket.) When we parted forty-eight hours later, neither of us could have denied it: a totally unexpected chain of events had begun in our lives and in our heads. Already, all bets were off.

The next time I saw him was about a month later, at my house in Texas. He was really anxious about meeting my kids; to both of us, Philadelphia seemed long ago. But our doubts dissolved when my sons reacted to him as if he were a hip, athletic Santa Claus. He paid so much attention to them I started to get jealous myself.

Six months later, we got engaged. It was a beautiful fall day in Seven Valleys, Pennsylvania, and we took his kids to school in the morning, then drove back through the countryside. We were looking at houses, idly of course, and he was talking about how he needed to buy a house for tax reasons, and he needed a tax consultant, and—

I made a frustrated noise somewhere between a sigh and a giggle.

"What?" he said.

"You don't need a tax consultant, baby," I said, unable to hold the words in check any longer. "You need to marry me."

There, it was out. By the speed with which the conversation progressed, it was clear we had both been thinking about this for a while. Within twenty minutes, we were on wedding details and names for a baby. By then we were at his house, and he stopped the car and told me that thinking about marrying me was making him feel like crying and it was also giving him a hard-on.

Which really was the most romantic thing I had ever heard in my life.

Later that day, we went shopping and found a little diamond solitaire, which was exactly what I wanted. Nothing creative or original, please, just the international symbol for I'm Getting Married! Then we went out to dinner, and when we got home, he actually got down on one knee and asked me to marry him. I was so breathless I could barely eke out a tiny "yeah."

A few months later, I was getting estimates from moving companies.

You know, I may not have sold many books that night last year in Baltimore, but when I consider that I might not have gone there at all, I catch my breath. What if our mutual friends hadn't told Crispin about the reading? What if

Crispin hadn't taken their suggestion, or hadn't waited, or hadn't had the nerve to send that e-mail of his own? When I think about the window of opportunity, which was so narrow, and the odds against it, which were so high, I have to wonder if, against all reason, there really is a Big Plan for Our Lives. I'm not the kind of person who believes in things like that. But the great thing about the big plan is that it doesn't care whether you believe in it or not.

I'm writing this from a study in the Pennsylvania countryside with my three-month-old baby girl sitting on my lap. Yet another love story has begun. Which reminds me: In sixth grade, my son took a survey of his class to see which age people think is the "best" age in life. It seems that these eleven- and twelve-year-olds generally agreed the best age would be around sixteen or eighteen. My husband and I laughed when we heard this, but we agreed that we've always felt as if the best age is right up there around the bend. Even now, it still feels like it's ahead of us. It must be really sad to reach the day when you believe all your good times are in the past.

On second thought, however, I started to see the survey differently. I remembered that when you're twelve, eighteen seems like forever in the future. Thirty is science fiction when you're twenty. The good times are so far away, they may never arrive.

Even if things seem to have worked out for me at this point, I certainly remember what impatience feels like; for me, it was always combined with a deep longing for love. Put them together and you get a wicked case of desperation, which was the fuel that sent me zooming around like a nut for so many years. I know every cure for this that doesn't work, and one thing that does. It's something like faith, though you might just call it extremely embattled optimism. Because it's definitely not a tranquil faith, a religious faith, or even a faith that anyone would recognize as faith. The feeling I'm talking about is a fierce, messy thing, a faith with gritted teeth and ADD. It has one prayer: Someday my fucking prince will come.

Poor dear brokenhearted people, I'm telling you because I know. You can't make someone love you. You can't make someone stay. You can, unfortunately, make them feel sorry for you and want to flee. And anyway, you don't want the love you have to chase down and hog-tie. One day, it will show up on your doorstep. All the love you can handle, waiting for you with a bouquet.

And that will just be the beginning of your story.

afterWORD

That night after the Spartan Scholars assembly, I went out to dinner with my mother and my sons. The restaurant we went to is a steak place now, but it used to be an Italian joint called Memory Lane. Visiting my high school had been a strange trip down that road. I had confronted my old self, that awkward prototype in the terrible gym suit who was so stuck in high school—and I think I got her out of there at last.

When I was a kid, I was always getting the advice "Be yourself!" whether from teen magazines or sympathetic grown-ups or cheery posters on the wall of the school cafeteria. So I would go ahead and do just that and it would blow up in my face. I'd be suspended from school, rejected, or misunderstood. Hey, no fair! I was just being myself, like you said.

I hope my seven rules are a little more useful version of that same counsel. These are the ways my friends and I actually learned to be ourselves, which involved first finding out who we were, then having the balls to stick with those self-concepts when things didn't work out immediately, as we would have liked.

It takes some flexibility. Back then, I wanted to grow up

to be something like Madonna: an outrageous, brilliant diva with a perfect figure and my own record label. Or my own television show. Or something like that. Wanting to be a superstar is fine, but eventually I had to redefine my goals in a more realistic way. I had to figure out what I was good at, and work hard at those things. And while at first I thought I didn't care what anyone thought of me, and later I realized I very much did, ultimately I came up with a weird blend of iconoclasm and conventionality that expresses who I am and how I fit into the world. It isn't Madonna, but it is me.

I hope there's something in here that helps you get to you, something that lights your crooked path or soothes your unruly soul. Sometimes a book contains just one sentence or one idea that stays with you a long time, that you keep in your head as evidence, as encouragement, as confirmation of what you really already know. If you found one of those in here, that would be good enough.

If not, there's this poem by Robert Frost . . .

Marion Winik
October 2000

ABOUT THE AUTHOR

Marion Winik is the author of *Telling*, *First Comes Love* (a *New York Times* Notable Book of 1996), and *The Lunch-Box Chronicles: Notes from the Parenting Underground*. A commentator on National Public Radio's *All Things Considered* since 1991, her essays and articles have appeared in *Redbook*, *Self*, *Cosmopolitan*, and many other publications. After twenty years in Austin, Texas, she now lives in Glen Rock, Pennsylvania, with her husband and children.